SASRA in the
Second World War

Eye-witness accounts
from the archives

EDITED BY BILL NEWTON

DayOne

MissionAssist
serving world mission from home

© Day One Publications 2020

ISBN 978-1-84625-670-7

British Library Cataloguing in Publication Data available

Joint publication with SASRA, Day One and MissionAssist

Day One Publications
Ryelands Road, Leominster, HR6 8NZ, England
Tel 01568 613 740
North America Toll Free 888 329 6630
email sales@dayone.co.uk
web www.dayone.co.uk

SASRA
Havelock House, Barrack Road, Aldershot, Hants GU11 3NP
Tel 03000 301 302   Fax 03000 302 303
Email admin@sasra.org.uk
web www.sasra.org.uk

Printed by T J International

Contents

Endorsements

There is a well-known aphorism that "when the lead starts flying there are few atheists in the trenches". This is a reminder that, while war is a terrible event, it often exposes men's need to find peace with God. It is then that men and women often "seek the Lord while He may be found".

This book makes prudent use of extracts from two organs (*Ready* and *The British Flag*) of former Christian societies which had amalgamated before the Second World War in 1938—"The Soldiers and Airmen's Christian Association" and "The Army Scripture Readers' and Soldiers Friendly Society". The author reveals the godly commitment and energy with which the evangelical world of the 1940s responded to meet the spiritual and practical needs of soldiers and airmen. The sacrificial provision of special huts and rest rooms for gospel work offered solace to many. The Scripture Readers of that generation, working with manifest support from Commanders and Chaplains, displayed courage, imagination and compassion in bringing Christ's gospel to servicemen and servicewomen in an hour of need. Many came to a living faith in Christ through these ministries.

Today's Soldiers' and Airmen's Scripture Readers Association have acted appropriately in producing *SASRA in the Second World War* to mark the 75th anniversary of the end of that conflict. Bill Newton and Phil Rush are to be congratulated for selecting material which will warm the hearts and minds of a contemporary Christian public. It is to be hoped that former servicemen in particular, who read these gripping accounts, will examine themselves to see if they are called today to participate in this worthy ministry in a field where in this generation the "harvest is plentiful but the labourers are few".

Brigadier Ian Dobbie
Vice President, SASRA

In a recent church meeting we were discussing our missionary support. The congregation's enthusiastic concern for the work of SASRA was as strong as ever. We love to hear of the work of the Scripture Readers, reaching out to anyone in the Services to see how they might help, and gently telling them of the one who helps most of all, the Lord Jesus Christ. This grand book will enlighten and inspire others in understanding the work of Scripture Readers so that people may be constrained to stand alongside our congregation (as well as hundreds of others) in their financial and prayerful support of humble, courageous men and women who are helping British soldiers and airmen in their own high and specialised vocations, and so committed to keeping us living in a safer world.

Rev. Geoff Thomas
Alfred Place Baptist Church, Aberystwyth

This is a fascinating book that compiles articles and pictures that give an insight into the work of Readers during WWII at home and abroad. It gives a glimpse of a very dark period in our nation's history and the sacrifices that were made during a time of conflict, but it provides a timely reminder that we have a great God who delivers, and who changes lives, and brings healing and hope even in the blackest and bleakest of circumstances. "He is the same and changes not, and is ever our Refuge and Strength." That same God continues to use SASRA to minister Christ to our forces in complex and confusing times.

Donnie G MacDonald
Moderator, Free Church of Scotland

I still have my SASRA lapel badge. I still count it a great honour to have been invited by the then General Secretary, Captain May, to join the ranks of those indomitable evangelists, the Scripture Readers. This book is twofold: their war record 1939-45 and their spiritual battlefront in winning service men and women for Christ. Both war-fronts required courage and tireless persistent commitment.

I also have imprinted on my memory from a few years after hostilities had ceased, sitting in Westminster Central Hall while full of service men, the fruit of Scripture Readers and others who laboured with them. One by one they came up to the microphone to give three minute testimonies, while Lieutenant General Sir Arthur Smith kept the troops moving, governing by drill numbers. National Service introduced me to Scripture Readers and we experienced, working together, more men turning to Christ than I was to witness for quite some years to come in my further years of service as an evangelist. Some called it Revival. We experienced great days together serving our Lord. What an example ASR William Scott was to me and so many others. Scripture Readers are the salt of the Earth. Jesus said so and I agree, certainly as far as these men and women are concerned. This record of their service in the war, and their ministry during peace time in winning service personnel for Christ, qualifies them for this title. Army Scripture Readers are amongst the best, down to earth personal evangelists with whom I've had the privilege of working.

This book is such an important record for me and many others of this great work for our Saviour Jesus Christ and is to His glory. May many more rise up in service for our Lord led by ASR's example and our prayer.

Roger Forster
Leader and Founder of the Ichthus Christian Fellowship

I commend *SASRA in the Second World War*. The account covers the familiar history of an international struggle to defeat great evil and recalls the dedicated service of 178 male and 20 female Scripture Readers who faithfully offered Christ, his grace and victory to service personnel. They did this through acts of kindness and heroism in huts, rest rooms, barracks and hospitals wherever there was need throughout the British Isles, Western Europe, around the Mediterranean and in the Far East. Countless lives were transformed by God's truth, and others were strengthened in their hope. The love of Jesus was offered to combatants and the defeated enemy through worship, friendship, literature and sharing from God's word. Our world still owes a huge debt to that unselfish generation. The modern church can learn much to shape our mission from this valuable account. Through the words of these brave Scripture Readers we are reminded of the spiritual needs and priceless value of every individual we are called to serve.

Rev Angus MacRae
Former Moderator of the Free Church of Scotland

During WW2 ASR&SACA, the predecessors of our own SASRA, grew to having around 180 Scripture Readers on active service both at home and overseas. The accounts of that vital spiritual work in this book, all drawn from archive records, demonstrate the importance of the work of the Association at a time when so many were being called to the service of their country and when so many paid the ultimate price. SASRA continues today to be uniquely placed to take the gospel "behind the wire" to service men and women, whose need is every bit as great as was that of the personnel in the Second World War.

Major-General Robert Thomson CBE DSO
Commander of British Forces Cyprus

The Second World War ended 75 years ago. The events of that momentous conflict have almost passed from living memory. Furthermore, our view of those times is often mediated through the lens of secular accounts.

Here is a story largely untold and unknown. It reminds us that God is, and that he is at work in the suffering, darkness and chaos of war. Through these first-hand accounts of SASRA Readers, we are reminded forcefully that God keeps his promises, and that he fulfils his purposes through the courage, faith and obedience of ordinary people who are surrendered to his will. We also witness in these pages the wonderful grace of God, in that Jesus Christ welcomes all, regardless of who they are or what they have done.

It is a thrilling read and brings with it the challenge of whether we in our generation are ready to spend and be spent for Jesus.

I heartily commend it to all.

Gerard Hemmings
Amyand Park Chapel

Foreword

It is a sad reflection on Man's inability to deal honourably with other human beings that only twenty-one years after the appalling tragedy of the First World War—supposedly so awful that it was to be the war to end war—Europe burst catastrophically into flames once again. Spreading rapidly beyond Europe, it sadly developed into a second World War, causing further tens of millions of fatalities and ending with the cataclysmic detonation of two atomic bombs. Our Heavenly Father must have looked on in sorrow at how Man was ruining His Creation.

But from tragedy and disaster can spring opportunity and hope. Whether the World or indeed Europe has really learnt lessons from the horrors of the Second World War it is hard to say. Nevertheless, those dark days brought moments of opportunity for Scripture Readers to bring the Word of God and the Peace of God to many who were prepared to stop, think and pray. There are few better-placed than soldiers to understand fully the tenuous link between life and death—a warm, sensible life abruptly ended by the explosion of a shell or the crack of a high velocity bullet. It is often said that there are not many Atheists in a foxhole. In the Second World War there were certainly many foxholes but, mercifully, many who found Christ when confronted by their imminent mortality.

In this remarkable short book is a most compelling account of how Scripture Readers, in support of Chaplains and working alongside other Christian soldiers, sailors and airmen, were able to bring many young men and women to a living faith in Christ. In their work in the field and in training camps and barracks, Scripture Readers were faithfully supported by their parent Soldiers and Airmen's Scripture Readers Association. The Association was itself supported, then as now, through prayer and sacrificial giving by hundreds of Church communities and thousands of individuals up and down our land. This book chronicles the activities of the dedicated cohort of Scripture Readers working amongst the men and women of our Armed Forces during the dark days of the Second World War who brought God's saving grace and blessing to many fighting for King and Country. But fighters need leaders, just as Christ led his disciples. In an extraordinary acknowledgement the BBC recognised that the lifelong SASRA supporter, Lieutenant General Sir William Dobbie, had led the defence of Malta with a Bible in one hand and a sword in the other. For the Scripture Reader, equipped with the whole armour of God, the Bible itself, as the Apostle Paul records in Ephesians Chapter 6, verse 17, is indeed the sword of the Spirit and the word of God. This book will be an inspiration to many who seek to follow in the footsteps of those who have gone before. The example of the Scripture Readers in the Second World War is truly one to follow as they pointed men and women to a living faith in the Prince of Peace.

Richard Dannatt
General The Lord Dannatt GCB CBE MC DL
President, The Soldiers' and Airmen's
Scripture Readers Association

1. Introduction

This book contains eye-witness accounts of SASRA's work during the Second World War. These have been drawn from its magazines (*The British Flag* and *Ready*) annual reports, Council minutes and other archives.

SASRA was formed in September 1938 by the amalgamation of:

- The Army Scripture Readers and Soldiers' Friend Society (ASR&SFS), which was founded in about 1838. It employed Army Scripture Readers (ASRs)—Christian ex-servicemen who initially went into barrack rooms to read the Scriptures to illiterate troops; and

- The Soldiers' and Airmen's Christian Association (SACA) which was founded in 1887 to unite those in the Army who were seeking to witness for Christ. Until 1920, it was known as the Soldiers' Christian Association (SCA), the name being changed to recognise the increasing work with the RAF.

Until June 1950, SASRA was known as the Army Scripture Readers and Soldiers' and Airmen's Christian Association (ASR&SACA). For simplicity, the name 'SASRA' has been used in this history.

The combined organisation was described in the October 1939 edition of *The British Flag*:

> The question is sometimes asked 'What is a Scripture Reader? and what is the ASR and SACA?' Space does not permit of a comprehensive reply, but the following points may help to give a picture of what they are and what they do:

(a) Originally the Association was two separate bodies, The Army Scripture Readers Society, having as its object 'To spread the saving knowledge of Jesus Christ amongst the personnel of His Majesty's Forces,' had been in existence for over 100 years and has endeavoured to provide Scripture Readers at Home and Abroad wherever troops are stationed in large numbers. The work of the Society was essential to get into personal contact with the men. They wear a uniform, are old soldiers (or airmen), are recognised by and work with the authority of the Army Council and Air Ministry, and goodwill of the Chaplains' Departments.

(b) The Soldiers' and Airmen's Christian Association had been in existence for over 50 years, its object being 'To bind together in the Love of Christ and Christian Brotherhood all who truly belong to Him.'

(c) These two great works were united into one Association last October [1938] with the result that the effectiveness of the work is increased whilst the cost of the work is reduced.

During the Great War[1] both the ASR and SACA did a great work. The former by extending their work at Home and Abroad and especially with the Expeditionary Force, some of the Readers working in the front line.

The SACA concentrated on providing Huts at Home and abroad at the various base Camps. These huts provided a great need as a place of refreshment for Spirit, Soul, and Body, and a work of personal evangelism was carried on throughout and indeed ever since the Great War, in an ever increasing circle of influence.

(d) The immediate aim of the Association is primarily to provide as many Readers as possible to meet the need at home and abroad, in barracks, camps, hospitals, troopships,

---

1   The First World War, 1914-18.

detention barracks and if need be, the Front Line of our fighting Troops, secondly to provide Huts at the Base Camps abroad and the Training Centres at Home.

These men need equipping in every way and the Huts have to be provided as well as equipment for them too, Harmoniums, Pianos, Bibles, Hymn books, tables, chairs, etc.

This book focuses on the main campaigns of the British Army and Royal Air Force. It refers to the Allies, as many counties fought alongside the British, and the Axis (Germany and its allies which included Hungary, Italy and Romania). Japan is referred to separately as, although an ally of Germany, there was relatively little collaboration.

Editorial comments are in boxes and footnotes. The rest of the text is from contemporary documents with some splitting of paragraphs, changes to punctuation, etc.

Wartime censorship meant that contemporary reports often did not include specific locations or the names of people and military units.

Acronyms are listed at the end of this book.

2. The Home Front (1939-45)

Timeline

1938

- 29-30 September: Hitler (German leader), Mussolini (Italian leader), Daladier (French Prime Minister) and Chamberlain (British Prime Minister) met in Munich, Germany.

1939

- 6 April: a defence agreement was concluded between Britain and Poland.
- 26 May: the British Military Training Act introduced conscription.
- 1 September: Germany invaded Poland.
- 3 September: Britain and France declared war on Germany.

1940

- 10 May: Winston Churchill became British Prime Minister.
- 10 July: the Battle of Britain began.
- 7 September: the Blitz (Axis bombing of London and other major cities) began. It lasted until April 1941.

1941

- 22 June: Operation Barbarossa—Germany invaded the Soviet Union.
- 11 December: Germany declared war on the United States.

1944

- 13 June: start of V1 flying bomb attacks on London.
- 8 September: start of V2 rocket attacks on London.

1945

- 26 July: Winston Churchill lost British General Election. Clement Attlee became Prime Minister.

Conscription

The Military Training Act of 26 May 1939 introduced a limited form of conscription. Only single men 20 to 22 years old were liable to be called up, and they were to be known as 'militiamen' to distinguish them from the regular army. The first intake was to undergo 6 months of basic training before being discharged into an active reserve. They would then be recalled for short training periods and attend an annual camp. At the outbreak of war the first intake was absorbed into the army.

SASRA made preparations to work with the conscripts.

'The Second Batch'
(From *The British Flag, January 1940*)

The Army Scripture Readers and Soldiers' and Airmen's Christian Association.

MILITIA

N.B.—If YOU desire CHRISTIAN FELLOWSHIP, please fill in and post as soon as you receive orders to join your Depôt.

SURNAME (Block letters) .... INITIALS...............
HOME ADDRESS ....
....
DATE OF POSTING........................ DEPOT STATION....................

Regimen-tal No.	Rank	Regiment	Denomi-nation	Remarks

Movements (for Office use) ....
....
....

Postcard used to identify Militia recruits
(From *Operation Logos*)

CONSCRIPTION

It was decided to make every effort to extend the work so as to reach effectively the men being called up as Militiamen.

The General Secretary reported having had preliminary conversations with the NYLC, Crusaders, Evangelisation Society and the LCM. There are 23 Depots with no Acting Readers[2] and 7 others which are inadequately served at present. It was decided that the General Secretary should continue his conversations with the above Societies with a view to definite proposals being made for effective co-operation in providing Acting Readers for these 30 Depots, and for interchange of information in regard to members with the Crusaders and NYLC so that members

---

2   Infantry Training Depots, with 200 to 250 men, were too small to warrant the appointment of a full-time Scripture Reader.

of these bodies reported for training would be notified to this office and contact made quickly with them on joining.

The following programme was approved:–

(1) Appoint Acting Readers for each of the 30 Depots mentioned above.

(2) Accumulate information in regard to the position of Militia Camps with a view to

    (a) Placing full time Readers for work there

    (b) Holding week-end Missions possibly by the YLC and

    (c) Holding longer Missions possibly by the Evangelisation Society.

(3) Institute a system of postcards with the Crusaders and YLC with a view to forming a card index of members in these organisations as they are called up.

(4) That the Church should be approached to make some announcement in their magazines asking members as they are called up, to place themselves in touch with the Association.

(5) That the Church Army should be approached with a view to possibly supplying workers.

The General Secretary reported

    (a) That in the conversations he had had with these organisations, there appeared to be a very definite desire to co-operate on the above lines.

    (b) Advertising. The advertisement for the front page of 'The Christian' on 25th May was submitted and amended. The General Secretary reported having been invited by The Christian to be interviewed by one of their Reporters for an article in regard to the steps being taken to meet the need of the Militiamen.

(c) The Chaplain-in-Chief to be kept informed of the plan and progress made.

Council Minutes, 17 May 1939

King George VI's broadcast to the nation

The September 1939 edition of Ready included the message broadcast by King George VI from Buckingham Palace throughout the Empire at 6 o'clock on Sunday evening, 3rd September 1939.

King George VI (reigned 1936-52)
(From *Ready, July-August 1942*)

"In this grave hour, perhaps the most fateful in our history, I send to every household of my peoples, both at home and overseas, this message, spoken with the same depth of feeling for each one of you as if I were able to cross your threshold and speak to you myself.

For the second time in the lives of most of us we are at war. Over and over again we have tried to find a peaceful way out of the differences between ourselves and those who are now our enemies. But it has been in vain.

We have been forced into a conflict. For we are called, with our Allies, to meet the challenge of a principle which, if it were to prevail, would be fatal to any civilised order in the world.

It is the principle which permits a State, in the selfish pursuit of power, to disregard its treaties and its solemn pledges; which sanctions the use of force, or threat of force, against the Sovereignty and independence of other States.

Such a principle, stripped of all disguise, is surely the mere primitive doctrine that might is right; and if this principle were established throughout the world, the freedom of our own country and of the whole British Commonwealth of Nations would be in danger.

But far more than this—the peoples of the world would be kept in the bondage of fear, and all hopes of settled peace and of the security of justice and liberty among nations would be ended.

This is the ultimate issue which confronts us. For the sake of all that we ourselves hold dear, and of the world's order and peace, it is unthinkable that we should refuse to meet the challenge.

It is to this high purpose that I now call my people at home and my peoples across the Seas, who will make our cause their own.

I ask them to stand calm, firm and united in this time of trial. The task will be hard. There may be dark days ahead, and war can no longer be confined to the battlefield. But we can only do the right as we see the right, and reverently commit our cause to God.

If one and all we keep resolutely faithful to it, ready for whatever service or sacrifice it may demand, then, with God's help, we shall prevail.

May He bless and keep us all."

God Save the King

Ready, September 1939

The King also recommended reading the Bible:

A MESSAGE FROM
HIS MAJESTY THE KING.

———

" *To all serving in my forces by sea, or land, or in the air, and indeed, to all my people engaged in the defence of the Realm, I commend the reading of this Book. For centuries the Bible has been a wholesome and strengthening influence in our national life, and it behoves us in these momentous days to turn with renewed faith to this Divine source of comfort and inspiration."*

15th September, 1939.

(INSERTED IN THE BIBLES ISSUED BY THE
B. & F.B.S. AND SCRIPTURE GIFT MISSION.)

> ### SASRA's War Policy
> Immediately after the declaration of war, SASRA's Council set out its War Policy.

A letter from War Office having been received inviting the Association to a conference 'to consider the means by which the various Philanthropic Organisations can best minister to the welfare of the troops in time of war and make recommendations', and in view of an offer from Mr J W Laing to erect four Huts and to supply the salary of an evangelist in each, the Council held a special meeting to consider the offer and to frame a War Policy.

(a) War against Germany having been declared on 3rd September the conference at War Office was postponed.

(b) It was unanimously resolved to gratefully accept Mr Laing's offer of four Huts or their equivalent of £4,000 which, if preferred would be given on the understanding that it would be expended on Hut work. It was also agreed that any other Huts or monies for the purpose that may be forthcoming, should be accepted.

(c) The Hut work was to be supplementary to and not take the place of the Association's present policy of placing as many Readers as possible in Barracks and Camps at home and abroad.

(d) No monies of invested funds must be used for Hut work

(e) War Office to be immediately notified and their sanction be asked to erect the Huts, and Mr Laing to be informed as soon as permission had been granted and sites selected.

Council Minutes, 4 September 1939

Members and Branches

SASRA's membership was organised into local branches. The following refer to the membership and branches.

There is a side of the work of the Association, which is not, perhaps, so well-known to our subscribers as is the evangelistic endeavours. It is the linking up of Christian men in the Forces with other Christians in the various stations.

Before the amalgamation of the two Societies, this work was mainly done by the Soldiers' and Airmen's Christian Association. Their object was 'to bind together in the love of Christ and Christian Brotherhood all soldiers and airmen who truly belong to Him.' To link up Christians in the Services with others of like mind means that instead of a separate witness in a camp there is a united front, which challenges the attention of the unconverted in a more forceful manner.

All Christians in the Army and Royal Air Force, may become Branch Members of the Association, and upon joining, receive a letter of welcome from the Secretary at Headquarters. They are encouraged to write freely of any difficulties and experiences which they may have, many of them do so. All the members in one Station form a Branch; each Branch has a Secretary who keeps in close touch with Headquarters, and arranges Branch activities for the members. It is obvious that the banding together of Christians in this manner must be of vital importance.

Each member is strengthened and contributes towards the strengthening of others.

Fellowship is essential in the lives of all Christians, and as soon as a Branch is formed an effort is made to establish a time for regular fellowship, so that members may be given opportunities for united Bible study and prayer. They are encouraged to read the Scripture Union portions daily, and at the weekly meeting the portions are discussed (with the aid of a black board), and given a practical application.

As may be imagined, it is not always easy for Christian men to find a place where they can meet for fellowship. Some stations and camps have Prayer Rooms and Soldiers' Homes, and in others Chaplains very kindly lend Church Rooms, but in many there is no meeting place available, and the men have to find somewhere themselves. In the fine weather they often hold their meetings out-of-doors, but otherwise they endeavour to secure a barn, or an NCO's bunk, or any corner of the Camp that is possible.

The surroundings, however, make no difference to the spirit of fellowship, and any place where such meetings are held becomes holy ground. Branches and isolated members are sometimes visited by the Secretary from Headquarters, and such visits bring cheer and encouragement, especially to those who find themselves alone.

The Association issues a monthly magazine, known as Ready, to help and encourage the Christian soldiers and airmen. It not only provides news of the various Branches, but also gives helpful articles which are intended to help them to grow in their Christian life.

In peace time the Association arranges annual rallies and week-end conferences for the men, and wherever these are possible they are warmly supported. Many members have received great help from the gatherings at Slavanka,[3] and others look back to visits to Keswick which have meant much to their spiritual lives. Every year, when possible, a Convention has been held in London, and here members from the different stations are able to meet each other; a Testimony Meeting is held, and helpful addresses are given. Where there are several camps in one area, such as Salisbury Plain, it is sometimes possible for the Christians to gather together for an afternoon, and such gatherings are always appreciated.

The British Flag, April 1941

What the war means to the Association we must leave our readers to imagine. So far as the Branch work is concerned we are already suffering dislocation, for almost every Branch has moved and individual Members scattered far and wide, nor for the time being are we allowed to know their whereabouts. In due course, however, we will look forward to receiving news from their respective fields of operation, and we know it will be to tell of His Grace having proved sufficient, and of strengthening in the inner man, owing to active service conditions having driven them closer to Himself and His Word.

Ready, October 1939

We are glad, however, to be able to say that, since the outbreak of the war, over 1,000 Soldiers and Airmen have joined the Association; most of these were Christians when they joined up, but many are hand-picked, the fruit of

---

3   Slavanka means "place of glory" in Russian. It was a Christian hotel and conference centre in Bournemouth.

the faithful labours of our Scripture Readers, oftentimes reaping where others have sown.

Ready, March 1941

Since the outbreak of war, 3,333 men and 166 women have joined the Branch membership.

The British Flag, July 1943

'Reader Fogell's Bible Class'
(From *Ready, September 1942*)

Branch Meetings were got under way and wherever we got three Souls registered for Christ we encouraged them to open a Branch. We still feel this is the Lord's method. He blessed His own work and we feel this is His Divine method. Encourage the members' witness in their own area.

Throughout 1944, the Branch work forged ahead. New Camp (RAF) averaged twelve at meetings. North Front (RAF) averaged eight. Windmill Hill (RA) averaged sixteen. Casements (Infantry) averaged ten. South Mole

(RASC) averaged eight. This is mentioned so that we may learn a lesson from Branches. These are the results of the Reader's visitation and we feel that these men would not have left their respective camps or billets, but would attend a meeting on the spot. There have been several spectacular cases, but how many were registered in the Lamb's Book of Life can only be known when the Roll is called up yonder.

Excerpts from ASR Cecil Fogell's journal,
Gibraltar 1943–44

SASRA's supporters

There were also local groups of Christians who supported SASRA's work. The following is from the 1940 minutes of the Felixstowe, Suffolk branch.

Several friends have been very active in the matter of enquiring (especially Mr A Edmonds, Chepstow Road) and endeavour to obtain a Hall or Room in which to open spiritual work amongst the forces; all available halls have however been taken over by the military authorities, and up to the date of the annual meeting of this branch on April 29th no suitable premises could be secured. Referring to this matter Miss D M Gorman (organising sec.) writes thus:–

> In a communication from HQ dated 2nd May, 'Keep on praying, I do believe God will soon answer, and send a Scripture reader. I have asked if the council will consider it at their next meeting (if they have one stationed at Bury St Edmunds he could visit possibly Ipswich & Felixstowe, there would then be three places to support him)': I will let you know more of this soon but in the meantime I feel our prayers should be concentrated not upon getting a room but having a reader.

A further communication dated June 3rd reads:–

> 'Please excuse the brief note you can imagine, I expect, how very busy national events have made us. Men are just pouring into the Camps: one Reader from whom I have just heard writes—Do please bear us up at the throne, it is just like being at the base in France. Thousands of wearied lads needing rest, encouragement and the Gospel. <u>Their tales of deliverance in answer to the 'Day of Prayer':</u>[4] of harassing weary miles of marching, bombed from place to place, are legion. <u>If ever prayer was needed for us it is now</u>.'

Huts

'The First Hut'
(From *The British Flag, January 1940*)

SASRA built huts at a several army and air force camps. Their use is explained below.

---

4   George VI called for a National Day of Prayer, which was held on 26th May 1940

Huts—The Council has gratefully accepted from Mr J W Laing,[5] the gift of four Huts and the support of their workers, with the desire that they will be used for the social and spiritual welfare of our Service men, and instrumental in winning many of them to Christ as was the case of our Hut-work both at Home and in France during the last Great War.

It is hoped that in due course other Huts will be erected in many concentration camps,[6] both at Home and overseas, but it will take some time to get such a scheme established. In the meantime we ask our Members to be much in prayer that the necessary funds will be forthcoming for the purchase of these and their maintenance, and also for consecrated men and women who will offer their services.

Ready, October 1939

On Tuesday, December 5th, the first of the Huts was opened in Blandford. At the opening and dedication service our Chairman, Brig.-General H. Biddulph, thanked those who had made the Hut possible, and the donor, who was present, expressed his pleasure at being able to do something for the men of the Services. The ACG Southern Command dedicated the Hut to the glory of God.

The Hut is for recreational and devotional purposes only, and it is hoped that every advantage will be taken of

---

5   John William Laing (1879-1978) expanded the family construction business into a national enterprise.

6   During the war "concentration camps" took on a very negative meaning. Here it simply means places where troops were concentrated before being otherwise deployed.

the facilities provided. It is intended to have Huts erected in other Camps at an early date.

Ready, January 1940

The hut is well built, lighted, and heated. It is in three divisions. The largest portion will hold 350 men at a meeting. Then there is a smaller 'quiet room,' where men can read, write, and where personal contact with the men is possible; and leading out of this quiet room are the quarters for the workers.

Many more Readers and Huts are required. Permission has been given for several more Huts to be erected, and others will be put up as soon as sites can be obtained, and the money is forthcoming to equip and maintain them.

The British Flag, January 1940

The Hut at Blandford is proving to be a real boon. The men are using it freely and say it is the cosiest place in Camp. Its Leader and those labouring with him are greatly encouraged. Writing recently, he said they had a record number attending the Meeting, the devotional room being completely filled, and some thirty in the recreation room remaining on for 'Family Prayers'. Many souls have been saved since its opening, and the Christian men cannot adequately express their pleasure at finding such a haven.

Ready, March 1940

A Bible Class has been started on Sunday afternoons. Some of the Christian lads have taken part, in testimony and in prayer, with something solid and helpful in the way of ministry of the Word to close with. Many have voiced their appreciation and encouragement. An echo was experienced last night when a lad sidled up to me and spoke of obtaining a glorious victory in the Barrack Room by kneeling at his cot to witness openly to Whose he is, and Whom he serves. I asked him what caused the exercise of mind. He said that although he was a Sunday School teacher in civilian life, it was when he came into the Hut and heard the bold and clear testimonies that he was urged by the Holy Spirit and conscience to come out openly for the Lord. We rejoiced together.

Quite a number have been helped by the entrance of God's Word, bringing light and liberty, pardon, peace and power. There are, I believe, hundreds of anxious souls in the Camp. Men who—if they knew what to do to be at peace with God, would do it—and some of these finding their way into the Hut through the Invitation Cards which go into the Barrack Rooms, with the printed Word of God, distributed by Mr Hall or myself, come seeking. Simple, straight ministry of the facts of the Gospel and the sweet appeal of the Saviour, and faces light up, eyes begin to shine—some with tears— and mouths are opened confessing the Lord Jesus as a new-found Saviour.

We are very conscious of someone praying for Blandford Camp, and if there is any success in the ministry of the Hut or in the Barrack Rooms visitation, and we believe there has been much success in both these avenues, then we give glory to God, and thanks and appreciation to all those who are, without doubt, calling upon our God continually for the work here. May this wonderful prayer support continue and abound more and more.

Ready, March 1940

Air raids

The German bombing campaign against Britain between September 1940 and May 1941 is known as the Blitz. Many cities were attacked and about 40,000 civilians were killed. Air raids continued at a reduced level throughout the war.

We desire to place on record our deep gratitude to God for His protecting care, so manifestly shown upon the lives of several of our Readers during the recent air raids. While Messrs Cirel and Mills, with Mrs Cirel were taking refuge in their dug-out, several incendiary bombs fell around them, one penetrating the roof, setting fire to the floor and to some chairs. Our brethren were able to get the fire quickly under control so that no further damage was done. As one of our friends aptly expressed it, it was 'through the Lord's goodness and in answer to prayer which had hardly reached Heaven'.

In another Station, Mr and Mrs Gibbon had an equally narrow escape, several houses around them being destroyed, while theirs received damage to roof, etc., they themselves were taking shelter inside underneath the stairs.

Ready, September 1940

Growth in the number of Scripture Readers

The rapid growth of the Army and RAF meant that there was a need for many more Scripture Readers. During the first year of the war, the number more than doubled.

In addition to ex-Servicemen, missionaries unable to return to their stations and other experienced Evangelists were accepted as Scripture Readers.

'Scripture Readers on Active Service'
(From the cover of a SASRA booklet)

When war broke out there were 65 Scripture Readers, to-day we have 150. That fact alone speaks for itself. Where best to place these Readers to get the utmost value is the concern of the Council at the present time. The vast increases in numbers of troops stationed in this Island which have come not only from all parts of the Empire, but also from European countries, offers a unique opportunity in the history of this Association. The earnest prayers of all our subscribers are asked that we may not be slow in seizing this opportunity and that the work may never be hampered or hindered through lack of prayer or funds.

The British Flag, October 1940

Rest Rooms

'The Rest Room somewhere in Ulster'
(From *The British Flag, April 1941*)

As the war progressed, the provision of 'Rest Rooms' became more important. Unlike the huts, they were rented premises which could be set up or given up at short notice as the locations of troops changed.

Thirty-five Rest Rooms were opened across the country. They were supported by an army of helpers who, despite the black-out, air raids and other dangers, spent long evenings at the rooms.

The ASR&SACA have started their first Rest Room in Ulster. The Opening Ceremony took place on Wednesday, the 11th December, in the presence of a large gathering, including five Scripture Readers.

The proceedings terminated with the Benediction and the singing of the National Anthem. Tea was served and some soldiers joined the company. Later about 50 men used the Rest Room for the first time, many of them remaining for the Epilogue Service.

The building is a commodious one, and a considerable sum has been expended in equipping it. So well has this been done that it should prove a real home to the members of the Forces. The townsfolk have been most generous in lending and giving furniture for the comfort of the men, and we are most grateful for their help.

The Rest Room is under the supervision of Reader Watson, who has done fine work for the Master among the soldiers. We will follow him with our prayers, that even a greater work may be done in this new place.

The British Flag, December 1940

Britain is full of troops. Every town is thronged with them and many a village, too. Marching, drilling, training, mounting guard they are kept 'at it' all day long—and how fit they look with their bronzed skins and developed muscles. Glorious lads from every quarter of the Empire—I counted no fewer than ten nationalities represented in one of our Rest Rooms the other day—they are a pleasure and inspiration to look upon. At length evening comes and a few hours of well-earned leisure; and here arises the problem.

How and where are they to spend the time? All are eager to leave camp or barracks or billet even if the only alternative is the street of the little town. But the nights are dark and cold and often wet, and the black-out adds to the gloom. Of course, there is the 'pub' at the comer and some men are quickly at home in such environment. But to a great number (possibly the majority) the bar is not familiar or congenial, and they find themselves there at first with reluctance, and commence the unaccustomed practice of standing drinks with a bad conscience. The local cinema absorbs many, but it is expensive, and not many can indulge except on pay-day at the week-end.

But what is this at the corner of the street? 'Soldiers' and Airmen's Rest Room' is attractively painted on the facia of what was formerly a large shop or warehouse. It looks inviting and proves more so within. Small café tables with chairs, a good fire glowing in the hearth, a canteen counter with tea and buns and cakes. Dart boards, ping-pong, papers and journals, and (by no means the least attractive feature) mailing materials for a letter home. Another room carpeted and furnished with arm chairs, settees and similar comforts. It is the quiet Room where men can sit and read and think and talk quietly through the evening.

What wonder such a place is hailed as a Home from Home by many a grateful lad who finds here not only creature comforts but a kindly Christian spirit vividly in contrast with the barrack room to which he will return. And the tender touch of 'evening prayers' with the loving Gospel message does not fail to give our Rest Rooms a distinctive character of their own which is their chief value. Overheard in the dark outside in the street, a soldier lad addresses a girl who is importuning him to spend the evening with her. 'No. I tell you I'm not coming out with you. I'm going in here to learn how to get my sins forgiven.' And in he came.

Hundreds of contacts are being made by our Scripture Readers every week within these Rest Rooms, and there have been many conversions. Not all are traceable at the time. Only the other day a Christian airman told me of two men who had come to Christ one Sunday night after a meeting in a Rest Room in a South-West country town months previously. Other cases are noted and rejoiced in at the time. On another occasion after a meeting, a Corporal sought the way of Salvation. He had lost both parents a few days before in a London air raid, 'and now I'm all alone in the world,' he told me. After leading him to Christ, I said, 'You must believe that He has received you in accordance with His promise.' 'I know He has,' he replied with a happy smile, and went away no longer 'alone in the world'.

Our Rest Rooms are springing up rapidly throughout the country. We have recently secured fresh places in North, South, East and West. All these should form important centres for evangelism and call for much prayer-backing by God's people. Our urgent need is for truly consecrated workers to take charge of centres as we secure them— men who know and love Christ and His Gospel and who understand men and love their souls. There is much land to be possessed and it is our ambition to spread the influence of this work throughout the length and breadth of our land wherever the fighting 'Sons of the Empire' may be found.

The British Flag, January 1941

It is now nearly a year since the ASR&SACA Rest Room in Edinburgh was opened and during the year many have appreciated the comfort and friendliness which they find there.

The position of the Rest Room is unique; it is situated in the main street, overlooking the beautiful gardens and the Castle. The comfort of the place is second to none. There is plenty of light and heat and a very good service in the tastefully decorated tea room with its small tables and dainty table cloths. Bowls of flowers add charm to the welcome, and often one hears remarks such as 'What a comfortable, homely place' or 'There is something different here.'

Those who work in the Rest Room are unsparing in their efforts to meet the needs of the men and women, most of whom are far from home, especially the men from overseas.

In the lounge on Sunday evenings one might see a sight which would gladden the hearts of many whose husbands, sons or daughters are in the Services. A meeting is held each week and the singing is very hearty. As these men and women choose their favourite hymns, one can feel that many of them are back again in the village chapel, the mission Hall, or perhaps in some church, where they sang in the choir, until their country called them. In the well-lit room, with the fire burning brightly, it is easy for the speaker to tell out the story of redeeming grace. Often after the service is finished, contact is made with someone who wants to hear more, and many there are who first answered the call of the Lord Jesus Christ in Edinburgh.

Other meetings are held during the week, and the Christian men look forward to times of happy fellowship in the Rest Room. To the Scripture Reader such a place is a real boon. It is a great help to know that there is a place to which he can invite men who are interested, and where, by means of a quiet talk, he can really help them.

The British Flag, January/February 1942

A German Pilot

About 900 German and Italian aircrew were captured during the Battle of Britain.

A German Pilot Officer with whom I have had many talks on the Bible when visiting Hospital, is as keen as ever to learn. He said that he recognises God's hand in his being brought down. Never before has he had an opportunity of hearing the Scriptures explained in the way he has heard since coming into Hospital. The Holy Spirit is teaching him, and opening his eyes to see the wonder of the Word. He said on one occasion that he was much struck with the fact that all my answers to his questions were taken from the Bible. A brother officer has been placed in the next bed to him, and he is now witnessing to this officer by passing on those things that I have been able to teach him.

Ready, March 1941

Incidents from the Battle of Britain

During the Battle of Britain (July to October 1940), the RAF successfully defended Britain against attacks by the Luftwaffe, Germany's air force. Between 13 August and 6 September, there were massive daylight attacks on RAF airfields.

'Spitfires off on Patrol'
(From a set of slides used by Scripture Readers)

'Can I see your pass, Sir?' This question asked by the new SP on the gate of the Drome[7] led to his saying, 'I'm interested in that, Sir,' as he read Air Force Scripture Reader on my pass. He was a Christian who had just arrived at the Station, and he was anxious for fellowship. Many happy times followed this meeting, times of prayer snatched at odd moments and

---

7   Short for Aerodrome

strange places, and Bible readings in the canteen, for we had no Church or Quiet Room then; but the great experience of his life came one day when least expected.

It was on a hot summer Sunday afternoon when Jack was on SP duty at the road barrier; all was quiet, and a lazy feeling lay over everything in the scorching sun. Suddenly the loud speakers gave warning, 'Action Stations!'

Jack was standing in his wooden sentry box with the road barrier in front of him, and a little village public house behind him, outside of which were parked several motor cars with a few civilians standing round. The ever-growing noise of aircraft caused everyone to seek shelter, but what followed happened so suddenly that most were caught unawares. Bombs dropped all around the little sentry box, machine guns rattled, and shrapnel whined and whistled; a civilian standing by Jack was killed, four people in an Anderson shelter[8] opposite were killed by a direct hit, the motor cars behind him burst into flames—a scene of unutterable confusion. Jack sat in his sentry box with splinters bursting through the sides and the glass of a hurricane lamp hanging on the wall falling all about him, but with a quiet peace in his heart—'I will say of the Lord He is my refuge'[9] running through his mind. All of a sudden a civilian, mad with fear, dashed into the box and buried his head in Jack's stomach, at which moment there was another terrific crash as a bomb exploded close by. Shrapnel flew, rattling all round, one piece hitting the civilian in the back! Jack was saved, but the civilian badly wounded.

8　Anderson shelter—a small prefabricated air raid shelter designed in 1938 and named after Sir John Anderson.

9　Psalm 91:2

I met Jack a few minutes later full of thankfulness to God for his protection. He was unscratched and unharmed. We walked up quietly to the canteen, and there read together the 91st Psalm, while Jack gave his testimony to his mates who gathered round—a testimony of peace through the knowledge of sins forgiven and protection and care in the moment and heat of battle.

Jack will never forget the day God fulfilled His promise—'The Name of the Lord is a strong tower; the righteous runneth into it and is safe.' [10]

Arthur loved his Bible; this was evident to all; any hot summer day when he was off duty you could see him sitting out in the sun reading it in full view of all who passed by. But Arthur found the need of going away for a quiet time with the Lord, and had found a quiet room in a block of bombed billets. Here, with the middle of the building a heap of ruins, he had found a room still intact, but empty, and at one o'clock every day he slipped away after lunch to seek the Lord.

This particular day, like many others, the time had come for this exercise, and away he went—but just as he was about to enter he saw one of his comrades who said that he had not been able to have his meal because of duties. Arthur wanted his quiet time, but out of Christian love he said, 'I'll stand in for you and do your guard on the gun post, while you have your meal.'

Then the unexpected happened, suddenly and without warning. Planes had been about all day; and the drone of another seemed nothing unusual; no warning was sounded, no guns fired, till the Dornier roared out of the bank of

---

10 Proverbs 18:10

clouds, dived with terrific speed and released its bombs. Whine, crump! Whine, crump! Down they came in a flash it was all over, hardly a gun having been fired. Arthur knew they had fallen near him; he had felt the blast, but just where was covered with a cloud of dust. Gradually it cleared, and there was the old bombed billet, now a larger heap than ever—the little quiet room where Arthur would have been just a heap of rubble. Arthur raised a prayer to the Lord Who had overruled the circumstances which on that particular day had caused him to give up his quiet time for his friend.

'The Angel of the Lord encampeth round about them that fear Him, and delivereth them' (Psalm 34:7).

'Action Stations!' These words over the Station loud-speaker were only too familiar in the Battle of Britain, followed so regularly with 'Take cover everybody,' 'Take cover everybody.' John came out of his billet and went to the underground shelter allotted to him, with many other men and some WAAFs. The shelter was a large one, and quite dark inside apart from the light that shone from the entrance. It was evident after a few minutes that this was going to be no usual raid; soon the guns started firing, and then the roar of aircraft was heard; they were dive-bombing the Drome, a seemingly endless stream. The earth trembled as bombs exploded; the shelter seemed all too insecure while death and destruction were all around.

There was a tense silence in the shelter, as the bombing went on for what seemed to be an endless age; then some men began to sweat, some were heard to pray who had never prayed before, and one of the girls was being comforted by another, when suddenly the ground heaved up under them, the walls of the shelter seemed to come in, and black darkness and choking dust mixed with the smell of cordite.

A 2,000 lb bomb had fallen on the entrance! John had been quietly praying for help and safety, and felt bewildered. Was his prayer unanswered? or are they all buried alive? or was he the only one left alive? Then oh! The wonder of it! He saw a glimmer of light coming from where the entrance had been, and, making his way to that end, he found a little hole just large enough to get his hand through. Soon he had enlarged it, and all crawled out one by one—Saved! John's prayer was answered, and now he knows the Word of God is true which says, 'Call upon Me in the day of trouble; I Will deliver thee and thou shalt glorify Me' (Psalm 50:15).

R E Ford.

Ready, November 1941

Work with the RAF

There was a large RAF presence in Britain throughout the war. The following is an example of SASRA's work with the RAF.

'A Hut for Airmen'
(From *The British Flag, October 1940*)

On a dark, winter evening two very dejected recruits of the RAF wandered down into a remote Welsh village. They had arrived in the neighbourhood only a few hours before, with the prospect of remaining for several months. At that moment it was an unpleasant prospect which the strangeness, the remoteness, the dampness, the darkness and the cold did nothing to mitigate. They were, in fact, not merely dejected, but were swiftly approaching the conviction that life was 'a poor show' and most of the standards and codes they had been taught to respect did not amount to much.

Seen in perspective, the situation is not without its humorous side. But at the time there was no humour in it at all, for the mood of the two men was a dangerous one—dangerous to themselves.

Previous enquiry had elicited the information that the village boasted a Services Canteen called 'The Airmen's Rest,' and that knowledge provided the one ray of hope to pierce the gloom which overhung their spirits and surroundings. But it was a hope inspired entirely by the prospect of obtaining a cup of tea and the warmth of a fire, and neither of these things—acceptable and necessary though they surely were—could satisfy the deepest needs of the two men.

The homely wooden hut was crowded. At one end, four figures were engaged in a game of table-tennis. Seated at tables, men talked, played games, drank tea and wrote letters. Others sat reading in armchairs, ranged each side of two large stoves. At the piano an airman strove manfully to compensate for a lack of musical ability with an over-abundance of enthusiasm. In front of the service hatch was a sizeable queue to which the newcomers attached themselves.

They were just two more airmen, two more blue-clad figures, entering upon a scene already dominated by such figures.

Then suddenly they became conscious of the kindly regard of a man who stood near the serving hatch. He, too, wore a blue uniform, but it was not that of the Royal Air Force. Having caught the attention of the two airmen, he stepped forward. 'Good evening,' he said pleasantly, 'you are newcomers, aren't you?' 'Yes,' they replied. 'I thought I hadn't seen you before. Well, make yourselves at home. There's tea and cakes, chocolate when we can get it, stamps, paper to write on and books to read. And—well, if you have any troubles, something you want to talk about, just come along and tell one of us, Mr ——— or myself. We are here to help in every way we can.'

It would require more than a few hastily written paragraphs to describe the valuable work performed by that small band of kindly Christian folk at the 'Airmen's Rest.' Suffice it to say that the initial welcome received by those two airmen revived their spirits and cheered them even more than did the very excellent tea and the warmth of the fires. In the months which followed, the 'Airmen's Rest' became their chief rendezvous. As one of them used often to say, 'We feel a hundred miles nearer home when we are at the "Airmen's Rest"'.

The story I have related is very simple and very brief, but immensely revealing. There was a great need and a danger. Someone strove sincerely to supply the need and avert the danger, and that 'someone' was not one individual but a small band of people, actuated by impulses and by a Spirit which offers the only real hope for stricken humanity.

The story of these two airmen is not an isolated one. The physical dangers of Service life are accepted and measures are adopted to avert them so far as possible. But the dangers which threaten the moral and spiritual well-being of a Service man, though less tangible, are as real and ever present as those which imperil his physical being; and too often no protective measures are taken.

Service life is so entirely different from civilian life, and the newcomer to the Services is very much like an untried vessel suddenly launched upon a rough and unknown sea. Fresh from the stabilising influence of a good home, many a youth has experienced a new sense of 'freedom' when he has joined one of the Services. At last—he feels—he is a man, doing a man's job; and too often he aspires to be 'as big as the other fellow,' no matter how spiritually and morally small that 'other fellow' may be. With older types there is frequently a sense of frustration and almost of hopelessness. Separated from their homes and loved ones, unable to pursue the interests and occupations which formed so great a part of their lives, such types tend to drift.

Knowing something of these men's problems, reactions and temptations one is the better able to appreciate the tremendous importance of the work performed by that small body of Christians in that remote village somewhere in Wales, and also by the organisation which they represent. For they offer not merely service and kindliness, but sincerity. Service and kindliness will attract a lonely man; sincerity will hold him. In short, there is anchorage.

The light that shone from the 'Airmen's Rest' on that wretched winter's evening was not such as to infringe the black-out regulations, but it was there just the same; and still it shines forth. And I know that so long as it does, it will act as a beacon indicating safe anchorage for many a new vessel setting out upon its voyage through the strange and sometimes treacherous sea of Service life.

JLH.

The British Flag, March/April 1942

St Nazaire raid

The St Nazaire raid (Operation Chariot) was an amphibious attack on the Normandie dry dock. The loss of this dock would force large German warships to return to Germany for repairs. On 28 March 1942, the obsolete destroyer HMS Campbeltown (built as USS Buchanan in 1919 and transferred to Britain in 1940) was rammed into the dock gates. It was packed with delayed-action explosives that detonated later that day, putting the dock out of service until 1948. Of the 611 men who took part, 228 returned to Britain, the rest were killed or became Prisoners of War.

By kind permission of the OC I was able to visit the Commandos fresh from St Nazaire; they were a delightful crowd of lads, making up their kits, as many had lost all. When they saw my Gospels they were delighted, and several came from other rooms in case I ran out of them before I could reach their quarters. After a general talk I was able to get a good number of heart to heart talks at the bedsides of those who were more interested.

Ready, July/August 1942

Shortage of paper

During the war, Britain depended on material brought by ship across the Atlantic. Petrol rationing was introduced in 1939. From 1940, other items, including food and paper, were also rationed. The Battle of the Atlantic (German attacks on Allied shipping) reached a peak in early 1943 with 108 ships sunk by U Boats (German Submarines) in February 1943.

We wish to thank all who have been remembering in prayer our need of sufficient paper for maintaining a regular issue of READY. All that is possible has been done and many officials who have been interviewed have shown every sympathy but to no avail. We have, therefore, been forced to resort to the present weight and texture of paper, and to forego a cover, to enable the usual 12 page edition of the magazine to appear. If the letters from our branches are not always as long as usual, or any item is omitted from time to time, we know our readers will accept this as inevitable.

As there is still a need for further economy, it will be a great help if Branch Secretaries, Soldiers' Home workers and others who are in the habit of receiving more than one copy will kindly inform us if they can do with less.

Ready, March/April 1943

Flying bombs

Over 8,000 flying bombs (V1 missiles, 'doodlebugs' or 'buzz bombs') were launched against Britain between 13 June 1944 and 29 March 1945. They carried a 1,870 pound warhead at about 400 mph. Many were intercepted by Allied aircraft or anti-aircraft guns. The most destructive V1 explosion was on 18 June 1944 when the Guards Chapel on Birdcage Walk (near Buckingham Palace) was hit during a service—121 people were killed. This was about ¼ mile from SASRA's office.

The Guards Chapel after the V1 explosion in June 1944

Also, over 1,000 V2 rockets (ballistic missiles) were launched against Britain between 8 September 1944 and 27 March 1945. They could not be countered by defensive measures.

It was with regret that we had to postpone 'OUR DAY'[11] to October 28th, without having time to give everybody due notice, or to explain the reason why, although we feel sure all will have understood that it was on account of the flying bomb menace, and will agree that the Council were very wise in their decision. We trust that the situation will have eased sufficiently to allow the Meeting to take place on the new date, but should that not be so. due notice will again appear in the 'Life of Faith', 'The Christian', 'The Harvester' and 'The Record'[12].

All at Headquarters have been deeply touched with the many assurances of sympathy and prayer that have been received from friends and serving members in regard to the flying bombs. We feel that we must record our gratitude to God of His sustaining grace and protecting care for while bombs have literally fallen all round us including those in the grounds of Buckingham Palace and the Guards Chapel, Wellington Barracks and another within a hundred yards of 'Havelock House'[13] the only damage sustained has been a few windows broken and one or two other minor details.

We cannot say, however, that it has been at all easy to carry on especially during the early weeks of the attack, but through it all His grace has proved sufficient. During these weeks some of the staff had to face leaving homes that had lost windows, ceilings, doors, etc. as well as travelling difficulties to and from office. For their loyalty

---

11 Our Day is SASRA's annual rally.

12 These were contemporary Christian newspapers / magazines.

13 This "Havelock House" was at 35 Catherine Place, Westminster. It was named after Major General Sir Henry Havelock (1795-1857).

and devotion to duty during this period there was a special Minute recorded expressing the Council's appreciation.

Our Printer and his staff were similarly affected. On one occasion, on arriving at his works he found machinery and type huddled together on the ground, a bomb having exploded not many yards away. It cannot be wondered at therefore that mistakes made in Ready, which are especially noticeable in the 'Notes on Rations' for the months of August and October and for which he and we apologise and crave our readers' indulgence.

Ready, September/October 1944

3. With the BEF in France (1939-40)

September 1939 to April 1940 is known as the 'Phoney War' as the British and French armies faced the Germans across strong border fortifications. This ended in April with the German invasion of Denmark and Norway, followed in May by the invasion of Belgium, France, Luxembourg and the Netherlands. By the end of June, all these countries had surrendered, leaving Britain facing an enemy-occupied coast stretching from the Arctic Circle to Spain.

Timeline

1939
- 4 September: British Expeditionary Force (BEF) started to deploy to France. By 27 September, over 152,000 British troops had arrived.

1940
- 10 May: the German army began to attack the Netherlands, Belgium and Luxembourg.
- 20 May: the German army reached the coast at Abbeville, France, cutting off the Allied forces in Belgium and Northern France.
- 26 May – 4 June: Operation Dynamo—338,000 Allied troops were evacuated from Dunkirk, France.
- 14 June: the Germans entered Paris.
- 25 June: an Armistice between Germany and France came into force. France was divided between the German occupied zone in the north and west, and a German dependent zone in the south administered by French from Vichy.

With reference to your letter of 28th November, I am commanded by the Army Council to inform you that they will be glad to avail themselves of your offer to send Army

Scripture Readers to France and to grant facilities for them to work among the troops.

The Council propose that the Readers should be treated as equivalent to Warrant Officers for the purpose of attachment to Sergeants' Messes, that accommodation should be provided, subject to the payment of a rental charge (to be assessed by the Director of Hirings, British Expeditionary Force) and that rations should be provided on a repayment basis.

I am to request that you will be good enough to indicate whether these proposals are acceptable to your Association in order that the necessary instructions may be issued.

Letter from the War Office, 22 December 1939

It has been the Association's privilege to send Readers to accompany the troops on Active Service in every major campaign throughout the past hundred years, and this war is no exception. Already ten Readers are in France, and it is a joy to learn from them that, though the going is hard, they are proving that the Gospel which they carry to the men is still the power of God unto salvation.

Ready, February 1940

We found the Army Scripture Readers busy at their posts and universally in favour both with the Authorities and the Chaplains and the men. They are making daily contacts with the troops in barracks, billets, and hutments, and already some have been brought over the line to the Saviour. Difficulties of many kinds have had to be faced, including billets, rations and transport but nothing has daunted them, and we found them everywhere full of hope and courage.

There is no doubt as to the responsiveness of the men as there is equally no doubt concerning the need. The absence of any gathering place where the Gospel may be preached is apparent everywhere. In some cases the men have not had facilities for attending a religious meeting for months. Church parades are in many parts impracticable, and where held are often irregular in time and voluntary in attendance. The various outside agencies have not yet succeeded to any extent in supplying the need, owing to great difficulties in erecting huts for want of material and labour. Yet where small gatherings have been possible the response has been full of encouragement and it has been our joy to lead several individually to Christ wherever such meetings have been held.

The Christian men are greatly in need of centres where they may make contact with others and foregather for fellowship. Some are giving a good witness among their comrades; often in an original and even in an unconventional manner. One Christian man I met was detailed to assist at the 'Wet Canteen' (where drink is served) but he was discovered presenting the customers with tracts and advising them not to touch the nasty stuff and was promptly removed and put on a more congenial job!

The British Flag, April 1940

Rest Rooms in France

Two Rest Rooms, in Nantes and St Nazaire, were rented and equipped for recreation and devotional use. The first was opened on Tuesday, April 9th, 1940, a month before the German invasion.

'The First Rest Room with the BEF'
(From *The British Flag, July 1940*)

The opening was performed by Colonel Siddeley, who said, 'It is a pleasure to open this Rest Room. Mr Howe has been fortunate in selecting this site, as it is the most central site in the town. The Officer Commanding is glad to open a place that will be for the moral and spiritual uplift of the men in this Station. The YMCA and the Salvation Army hope to work here also.'

The British Flag, April 1940

On the opening day of one of the Rest Rooms, a soldier was heard to say: 'This is the first touch of home life we have seen since we, have been in France.' We trust all these endeavours to make our comrades' lives more pleasant while 'doing their bit' in France and elsewhere, will be owned of God and result in large numbers being 'born again,' thereby becoming inheritors of the Home Eternal.

Ready, May 1940

Working with the BEF

Ten Scripture Readers were sent to work with the British Expeditionary Force (BEF) in France. This is a typical account of their work.

The French YMCA helped them to find men in the scattered billets.

It was a miserable wet night when we set out to walk the two miles to camp. We had already received a wetting, and we were wondering whether we should wait until the rain ceased or eased off, then we remembered that we must 'sow beside all waters'[14] so we started out for Camp. Along the road we met groups of Militiamen who insisted on saluting us. However this gave us an opportunity to explain who we were and to preach the gospel to them. They were very attentive and thanked us. When we entered Camp we made for a hut which was filled with Militiamen who had just come across. From the start the power of God fell upon these men as we unfolded the way of salvation to them. An old soldier tried to cause a diversion but he was soon muzzled by the power of God.

The young fellows listened with rapt attention as we made known to them what it meant to be a Christian. Then we asked, 'Is there any here who will accept Christ?' One man coloured up and we felt he was going to yield but he moved away, we believe, under deep conviction. Before we left we invited any who wanted a further talk to follow us down the road. We left the hut sliding and slipping through inches of mud and water. We hadn't gone far when we were conscious of being followed. We turned

---

14 Isaiah 32:20.

to see a young fellow behind us. He said, 'I would like to accept Christ, will you help me?' We stood in the mud with the rain coming down on our bared heads, while he made his confession of faith in Christ. We had wings to our heels as we walked the two miles back to our billets.

Ready, May 1940

Evacuation

The German invasion split the BEF in two. Those North of the River Somme were pushed back to Dunkirk whilst those further South were evacuated through Channel and Atlantic ports such as Le Havre, Cherbourg and St Nazaire (about 144,000 British servicemen were evacuated from these ports).

None of the twelve Scripture Readers serving with the BEF lost their lives or suffered anything worse than loss of possessions. Whilst a few were evacuated through Dunkirk, the majority were South of the Somme. This is the account of one of these Scripture Readers. He referred to the danger of German air attack on the ships. On 17 June, the troopship Lancastria was bombed near St Nazaire with an estimated 4,000 killed, the worst maritime disaster in British history.

SS Lancastria sinking off St Nazaire

On Saturday, June 15th, there were many rumours that all Britishers with the BEF must leave their Stations. By 9 pm it seemed to be true, but no official intimation had been received, so I went along to the SCF for confirmation, and found him entering his car to pack up. When asked if the news was true, he replied, 'Very true, and I strongly advise you to get away South to a port of embarkation for the first available boat to England.' I said, 'Yes, but how?' He answered: 'Tack onto anything you can get, and as an old soldier you should know how to get away!' Forty-eight hours' limit had been given to clear out of France, and nine of those precious hours had already gone.

Our small party of Scripture Readers got together, and decided to get away early next morning. On our arrival at the railway station we were informed there were no trains running, and enquiry at the Town Major's office brought the reply, 'We have no transport.' We then urged that we must get away, by order. We were then told, 'All right, get your kit—just what you can carry in your hand—and be ready outside. I will stop the first convoy coming through and try to get you on it.' We had just returned with our kit when the remains of a Royal Artillery unit came along. We were quickly placed on a Bren gun truck, and after being lined up in the local football field for some time, we moved off, feeling an element of safety among the 'Gunners.'

The congestion on the road was intense; it took us 6 hours to travel 25 miles; we were then turned into a big car park for the night. An all-night disturbance from German 'planes going over to bomb a port 5 miles farther on, made us wonder if we would get away after all. 4.30 am found us having a wash in a field, chilled to our very bones, and with a deep longing for home, and at 7.30 we moved off under the protection of the Staff Officer. Again the conditions were so acute that we were four and a half hours travelling 4 miles! We arrived some 2½ miles from the embarkation point, and there turned into a large field into which we were packed like sardines in a tin. We then scrambled out of our transport vehicles, which had to be burnt before the enemy arrived!

And now we were supplied with rations. The old soldier instincts, born of long experience, proved invaluable. Listening to orders given, we caught the sound of a promise to the Colonel of a lorry to take the officers' kit to the boat. Immediately we offered to help load the baggage, and in due course we were all aboard the longed-for boat!

The voyage was a remarkable one! The tug landed us on a sandbank, the boat shivered from stem to stern, and sprang a leak. The tug then unhooked and made off, and appeals to other tugs failed to bring us any help; we could not get off. An order came from the Port Authority saying that we must get clear away out to sea by midnight, or be interned. With only fifteen minutes left in which to get away, the tide carried us off. It seemed that the Lord sent the tide in before it was due; certainly we got clear before the appointed time, and we were saved. But with a leaking boat, and a bomber overhead, it was still a most anxious time.

When daylight arrived we were going dead west, but where? There was much speculation, for no land was visible. When the boat's course was altered, there was more excitement. 'Planes overhead, guns barking, and an order for every man to get out of sight and all kit to be covered, all added to the interest! We were being chased by enemy submarines. Our Captain took a zig-zag course,

British and French naval boats scoured the seas, and, by God's grace, we pulled through. That night a gale sprang up, and this intensified the Captain's anxiety. We were all most uncomfortable, for the weather was now very cold, and our limbs were aching. On the following day no land was visible until about 2 pm, when it became evident from the boat's course that we were nearing Land's End. How we praised God for His deliverance! At 6.30pm we reached Plymouth Sound, and the next day were taken ashore in tenders, landing to the strains of the Royal Marine Band. We reached London early the next morning, tired, unshaven, and dirty—but intensely grateful to God to have been spared to serve on in the great work to which He has called us.

Ready, July 1940

Witnessing to survivors from Dunkirk

'Evacuation from Beaches'
(From *The British Flag, October 1940*)

In the hospital three men were side by side in the ward, and the remainder of the beds were empty. Two of the men were soldiers and the other a sailor. The sailor and one soldier had been at Dunkirk. After a long talk to the three of them, one soldier asked for a Gospel. He said that he had been given a copy by a Chaplain but had lost it with most of his belongings at Dunkirk. When I had given him another, the sailor asked that he might have one also. I remarked that the soldier in the middle bed did not ask for one, and he said he was an atheist. The sailor said to him: 'Were you with the BEF?' 'No.' Both men who had been at Dunkirk told him that had he been there, he would not have been an atheist, for most men cried to God to help them.

Ready, August 1940

Signalman X went out to France a puffed-up young man, full of his own ideas and thoughts about God, and lived his own life, wrapped up in high-sounding words, and vague conceptions of 'scientific theories.'

Then came the big push, and with it, applied science all around him, in the form of high explosive shells, tanks, aeroplanes, etc., and he found that there was very little constructive comfort in 'Science.' Later he found himself in utter helplessness, on the beach at Dunkirk, with others around him being blown into eternity and not knowing just when his turn would come. He sought for comfort in his atheism, there was none for him there, and in agony of soul he cried to the living God for deliverance. God answered the cry and the lad was delivered.

He arrived at our hut, a firmly convinced man, definitely believing in the existence of God. His trouble, however, was not yet completely dealt with, and he told me that he could not conceive that the God whom he knew, and the God of the Scriptures were one and the same, and that God had manifested Himself in flesh, and dealt with our sins on Calvary. I quietly asked him if he would seek a quiet corner, and take a copy of John's gospel with him, and ask God to teach him the meaning of the book. He came back the next night, and the light of heaven was in his face, as he told me that he was now believing that Jesus Christ was the Son of God and that he now understood. It was delightfully simple to point such a one to the Lamb of God which taketh away the sin of the world.[15] Surrounded by a swirling mass of battle-stained lads in khaki, we just bowed our heads and hearts before Him, Who is plenteous in mercy.

The British Flag, October 1940

---

15 John 1:29.

Testimony of a British Prisoner of War

'In a Prisoner of War camp in Poland'
(From *Ready, July-August 1944*)

About 41,000 British servicemen were missing or Prisoners of War (PoW) at the end of the 1940 campaign in France.

As an Ambulance Driver I was with others making my way towards Dunkirk with a load of wounded men when the convoy ran into a German ambush, and we were taken prisoner.

I was sent to a French Prisoners of War Camp in Alsace-Lorraine, and it was five months before I saw another Englishman. In the following October 1,200 fellow-British Prisoners of War came to the Camp presenting a saddening sight, unwashed, tired, and in many cases ill from weakness.

As soon as the Camp settled down Church Services were started; but as there were no chaplains these were carried out by the few men who felt the need of a Gospel witness.

Just before Christmas 1940 the Camp split up, and the section to which I belonged was sent into the Black Forest area. It was intensely cold, and as Red Cross supplies had not yet reached us, many men suffered greatly from malnutrition and frost-bite. It was under these conditions that my first Christmas was spent as a Prisoner of War, the memory of which will live as long as I. In the afternoon of that Christmas Day I saw a sight which was sublimely touching. The men were gathered together in a stable, which had been converted into quarters, and there, hungry and shivering with cold, they sang the songs of Him Who was born in that other stable so long ago. Many eyes were misty on that day as those men, separated from their dear ones, sang of Him Whose love is inseparable from those who trust Him.

Moving on through various Camps I found myself eventually in Poland, and with 19 others I joined a Camp which had been established for six months, but which had no Gospel witness of any kind. After much prayer I approached a new arrival, whose quiet consistent life had attracted me, and suggested that something should be commenced, to which he readily agreed, saying that he too had been praying on similar lines, and having obtained the necessary permission we started our meetings, with great trepidation believing that God would undertake. We had neither books nor music, but one man unearthed a copy of 'Scottish Hymnal for Soldiers' from which we copied the most popular hymns on to the blackout blinds with chalk.

Another move brought us to one of the largest Camps in Germany, where there were five chaplains of various dominations, and Church of England and Free Church Services were held on alternate Sundays, both morning and evening. There was one Sunday meeting, however, which we had all to ourselves started originally by a few Christian men as a Prayer Meeting; we were called the 'Three O'clockers!' Officially no preaching was allowed, but we could pray, sing, read the Word and pass on in a few sentences the Message of Life. What grand meetings they were! Many denominations gathered from widely scattered parts of the world, Australia, America, Canada, England, New Zealand, Scotland and Wales being all represented in the accompanying photograph.

I look back on those years as a Prisoner of War with thanks to God, for it was as such that I came to realize His love and power in a way that otherwise might have been impossible.

Ready, July/August 1944

4. North Africa, Middle East and Crete (1940-43)

Timeline

The campaign in North Africa has been likened to a swinging pendulum as one side and then the other gained the advantage—the front line moved hundreds of miles. There were few natural obstacles to defend and the battles often depended on the availability of troops, equipment and supplies.

1940

- 10 June: Italy declared war on Britain and France. Italy had forces in their colonies which included Libya, Eritrea and Abyssinia (Ethiopia), threatening the British in Egypt, Sudan and Kenya.
- 13 September: Italian army advanced cautiously to Sidi Barrani, Egypt.
- 7-9 December: Allies captured Sidi Barrani, taking about 40,000 prisoners.

1941

- 6 January: Allies captured Bardia, Libya, taking 45,000 prisoners. By 9 February, the Allied advance had reached El Agheila (about 300 miles into Libya).
- 12 February: Erwin Rommel arrived in Libya to command the German Africa Corps.
- 7 March: Allied troops started to land in Greece (re-deployed from North Africa).
- 24 March: Axis victory at El Agheila, Libya. By 11 April the Allies were back in Egypt with an outpost at Tobruk, Libya.
- 6 April: Axis invasion of Greece.
- 28 April: Allies started to evacuate Greece.
- 20 May: German paratroops assaulted Crete. By 30 May, Allied forces had been evacuated or surrendered. Three Allied cruisers and six destroyers were sunk.
- 21-23 November: Battle of Sidi Rezegh—Allied victory, Tobruk was relieved and the Axis forces retreated.

> **1942**
> - 21 January – 4 February: Axis offensive pushed Allied forces back across Libya.
> - 26 May – 21 June: Battle of Gazala (near Tobruk, Libya)—Axis victory, the Allies withdrew into Egypt.
> - 1 July – 11 November: Battles at El Alamein, Egypt—the Axis forces were held (1-27 July and 30 August – 5 September) and then defeated (23 October – 11 November).
> - 8 November: Operation Torch—Allied landings in Vichy French Morocco and Algeria.
>
> **1943**
> - 7 May: final Axis forces in North Africa (Tunisia) surrendered.

In the beginning of 1940 Mr Howe, who had been much blessed in his work amongst the troops in Egypt, returned home on completion of his term of service. In April reinforcements were sent out consisting of Mr J S St.Clair as Superintendent of the Association in the Middle East, with Messrs A V Oates and A Freeman Scripture Readers. In each of these countries Huts are in the process of erection.

Ready, Annual Report 1939-1940

On the same day [4 August 1940] we also despatched Messrs Howe, Wigg and Phillis to Egypt, making our Readers with the Forces in the Near East to number seven in all, five in Egypt, one in Palestine and one in Gibraltar. Each and all would say: 'Brethren pray for us.'[16]

Ready, September 1940

---

16 1 Thessalonians 5:25.

ASR's Desert Car

'The New Lorry for the Western Desert'
(From *The British Flag, October 1940*)

The Desert car with, from left to right, the driver, Major General Arthur Smith, ASR St.Clair (Superintendent in the Middle East), a Corporal in the Scots Guards and Rev A J Wilcox, the Assistant Chaplain General (ACG) Middle East.

We are indebted to The Honourable Mrs Arthur Smith for kindly sending us this photograph; she brought it home from Egypt after a journey lasting seven weeks, by river, rail, road, air and sea. It depicts our desert car, which has been designed to overcome some of the special difficulties of desert travel. The equipment includes awnings to shade the windows, an extra set of desert tyres, mats to roll out in front of the wheels should the car get stuck in soft patches, and also a set of metal tracks carried on the roof for the same purpose, a condenser (under near-side lamp) to catch all available steam, and cool it down to water again, so as not to lose a drop of precious moisture in a waterless desert. There are cupboards inside for Gospels and other religious literature. The equipment also includes a Wireless set which will attract the troops, and some petrol tanks to carry cold drinks for the men.

This travelling 'pulpit' was dedicated to the service of the Lord Jesus Christ by the Assistant Chaplain General, Middle East, the Rev A J Wilcox, who has always shown a most sympathetic interest in the work of the Association, and to whom we owe so much for enabling us to send to Egypt and Palestine, Mr St.Clair and his noble band of five Scripture Readers. By the time this appears in print, it is hoped that this modern 'chariot' will already have been used as a means of pointing many a soldier to the same Jesus to Whom Philip had the privilege of pointing the Ethiopian eunuch[17] (in that other desert, nearly two thousand years ago) and with the same result. This enterprise, in the Name of the Lord, is largely due to the good offices of our Vice-Chairman, Major General Arthur Smith, who, as our Readers no doubt know, has for many years been closely associated with the ASR&SACA.

Ready, October 1940

Since I wrote you last, I have been out in the van to the Western Desert. I enjoy the work immensely. The response to the Gospel messages have been amazing. Every night, after listening to the news, there is an earnest Gospel talk, and many men have come to know and love the Lord Jesus Christ through our visit. A young fellow whose friend

---

17 The Ethiopian eunuch's conversion is described in Acts 8:26-39.

had been killed by a bomb the day before said, 'I want to know how to be saved,' and in a trench he found the Lord Jesus Christ as his Saviour. We conducted sing-songs inside and outside desert canteens, talked and ate in the dark, had to break off to rush into trenches, because of air-raid warnings, taught choruses to men gathered from their guns and observation posts, and cooked meals. All this, with personal work, has occupied the days and nights in the desert, but the joy of helping these men to get to know the Saviour, sharing something of their hardships, and enjoying fellowship with other Christians, has been wonderful. On our last morning two men came and asked for a Testament each, and said they wanted to be saved. It was easy to point them to Christ.

The men nicknamed the bag of tracts 'The Ammunition Bag,' and they readily accepted tracts. Men in single dug-outs and in groups, even as they sat near their small dug-out canteen drinking, and on the seashore, all showed an interest in the message we had come to give them. One night after a ten or fifteen-minute talk in the dark to a party of men, the Commanding Officer, who had stood and listened with his junior officers, expressed his appreciation for our visit, and asked himself for a gospel.

These men are hungry for something which no canteen or mere van can give them. What wonderful opportunities there are, and we know the Word sown will come back not void, but accomplishing the thing whereto it was sent.

The British Flag, January 1941

Seeing me plod through deep sand in their camp, and not being familiar with the ASR uniform, two men (recently arrived from England) questioned me as to my right to be there. Having set their minds at rest I said, 'Now it is my turn to ask you a question. Can you tell me the way to Heaven?' After some floundering, they admitted that they could not, though both hope to get there, and so for a few minutes I told them of Him Who is the Way, the Truth and the Life,[18] and earnestly advised them to follow Him.

Ready, May 1941

Crete

At about 08:00 on 20 May 1941, about 3,000 German parachute troops landed on Crete supported by heavy bombing. By the 26th the British commander saw the position as hopeless and between 28th and 31st the Allies evacuated as many people as possible. About half of the island's defenders were killed or captured.

Mr F A Howe writes

One day I was asked to visit the anti-aircraft position and so went up to see the Gunners in the gun pits 12 miles away. That day the parachutists dropped. I was cut off but continued to work amongst the men—it was wonderful going into action with them against enemy aircraft. Four men were wounded. I helped to dress their wounds—took a lump of shrapnel out of a fellow's side. That evening the men gathered round and we had prayer and a talk in the gun pits.

Next day the Germans found our position and straddled us with six bombs—praise be, no casualties, though I was buried in dirt. Next day the way opened for me to get away, and so, running the gauntlet from a

---

18 John 14:6.

sniper, I got back to Canea[19] to find it flat. Our house had not been hit. I went back and forward to hospital—got caught in the valley by a German plane which machine-gunned the valley—hid in a cave for two hours, went on to hospital and from there never returned, I got cut off. Worked in the operating theatre with the surgeons—extracting bullets, taking out a fellow's eye, wiring up a German's broken jaw—visited the wards while heavy bombing was going on, cheering the men, all by God-given strength.

Next day we evacuated nearly all of our wounded, as the bombing was too much. Next night I took up a party of wounded to a place called Kleber and again got cut off—went on to Leon Koreon, about 5 miles away and that night we made a journey through the mountains of about 38 miles with a truck load of wounded. I lived for two days under a culvert in the road and then in the olive groves. Jerry machine-gunned us and bombed us for four solid hours. At last we made a dash for the beach. Weary and washed out I carried a wounded fellow down the river bed but finally had to get others to help. I shepherded the wounded on and then at last—washed-out rag as I was—boarded the boat. I mercifully fell asleep. About 100 miles out Jerry bombed our boat and killed 12 of our men. At last Alexandria.[20]

Ready, September 1941

---

19 Canea / Khania / Chania is near the west end of the north coast of Crete.

20 He was evacuated from Spahkia / Sfakia / Chora Sfakion on the south coast of Crete to Alexandria in Egypt.

Death of F A Howe

Frederick Alfred Howe (who served on Crete—see above) was the only Scripture Reader killed by enemy action during the war. He was travelling back to the UK on the British troopship SS Laconia when it was sunk by German Submarine U156 off the West African coast on 12 September 1942. He was 36 years old.

'ASR Howe on Mount Zion'
(From a set of slides used by Scripture Readers)

'MISSING'—FREDERICK ALFRED HOWE

For some months past the Council have been anxious regarding the well-being of our Reader, Mr F A Howe, who left Egypt in July last on being invalided home.

We regret to announce that official news is now to hand that the ship on which he sailed was 'sunk by enemy action,' and as his name cannot be traced in any list of survivors, it is presumed that he must be included amongst the military personnel with whom he sailed officially reported as 'missing at sea.'

All who have followed the career of our brother since he became a Scripture Reader in 1935 will remember how zealously he pursued his 'high calling of God in Christ Jesus',[21] and we would like to think of him being so engaged right up to the last, for we are sure he would have had on his heart the spiritual welfare of his fellow-passengers.

On three separate occasions during the present war he suffered the loss of all his worldly possessions, 'taking the spoiling of his goods joyfully':[22] the first was on the occasion of the evacuation from France with the BEF in 1940, following which he immediately volunteered for the Middle East, from which he had only just previously returned, having spent three years there, including some months with the troops on active service in Palestine, prior to the outbreak of the present war. From Egypt he accompanied the BEF to Crete, where he had some remarkable experiences and opportunities for Christian service some of which he so aptly recorded in our booklet, 'Then the Planes Came.'

On being evacuated from Crete he returned to Egypt, and was almost immediately involved in a motor accident in which he received head injuries which necessitated his having to lie in hospital for five weeks or so, from which he had not long emerged when nearly the whole of his belongings were destroyed in a flood which visited his camp.

It is not for us to reason why such a young and useful life should eventually so be cut off after coming through

---

21 Philippians 3:14.
22 Hebrews 10:34.

such vicissitudes, but rather, to submit to the One Who doeth all things well; we thank God for having loaned to the Association such a one who was ever found about his Master's business.

Mr Howe was unmarried, but he leaves a sister and brothers whom we commend lovingly to the God of all.

Ready, March/April 1943

The 'swinging pendulum' in the Middle East

In January 1942, the Axis launched an offensive which swept the Allies back over 250 miles across Libya. In May, a further Axis offensive pushed the Allies back over 300 miles into Egypt.

In the Middle East, too, where the campaign has taken on the form of a swinging pendulum, the leaders and the men under their command may depend upon our prayer support; such a turn of events must involve real disappointment, as well as a call to endure fresh hardships and privations, mingled with the possibility of loss of life or limb. May each and all experience in a large measure the Lord's sustaining grace, and buy up every opportunity of being a truly Christian witness, looking 'unto Jesus, Who for the joy that was set before Him, endured the cross, despising the shame, and is set down at the right hand of God',[23] in anticipation of that glad day when war shall be no more, and 'the kingdoms of this world are become the Kingdoms of our Lord and of His Christ, and He shall reign for ever and ever'.[24]

---

23 Hebrews 12:2.

24 Revelation 11:15.

We are now able to state that Readers J Bredin and C W Morriss[25] are on their way to Egypt and Palestine respectively, and that F Agnew has been posted from Egypt to Malta. While we continue to pray for our Readers overseas, let us not fail to remember also their wives and families, and other loved ones from whom they are separated, for the Gospel's sake.

Ready, March/April 1942

Malta

Malta was a key Allied base, potentially controlling the Axis supply routes between Italy and North Africa. It was under siege by the Axis air forces between June 1940 and November 1942. About 30,000 buildings were destroyed or damaged.

Lieutenant General William Dobbie (1879-1964), was Governor and Commander-in-Chief of Malta between April 1940 and May 1942. He was a keen supporter of SASRA, for many years been a member of the Council and was Temporary Honorary Director before his appointment to Malta.

'General Sir William and
Lady Dobbie
on their arrival from Malta'
(From *The British Flag,
July-September 1942*)

---

25 C W Morriss died on 9 November 1943. The British Flag for January/February 1944 recorded: 'It is with deep regret that we have to record the death in hospital in Palestine of Scripture Reader C W Morriss, and we extend our deepest and prayerful sympathy to Mrs Morriss and the family in their sad loss.'

Our prayers are continually with those who are bearing the brunt of the war in Malta and the Middle East. In the former place, General Sir William Dobbie has evoked the admiration of all by his dogged determination to uphold the highest traditions of the British Army and qualities of Christian leadership. Readers will remember the description, given by the BBC, of his defending Malta with the Bible in one hand and the sword in the other.

The British Flag, March/April 1942

Work on a troop ship

Once Italy entered the war, troop ships between Britain and Egypt had to sail round South Africa rather than taking the much shorter route through the Mediterranean. This gave Scripture Readers much longer contact with the troops.

Some of our Readers have recently left for the Middle East and India, and we have received very encouraging reports of how God has been blessing their work amongst the Troops on the voyage out. One of them writes:

Opportunities for service on board soon arose. A young sailor was attracted to the cabin on the first Sunday when I was playing my accordion, and poking his head inside the porthole he made himself known. Later on, he brought a bombardier, a member of the SACA. That evening we had two or three in the cabin for a read of the Word and prayer.

Each evening the numbers grew until we packed fourteen men into our little cabin which only boasted of one chair, but the fellows didn't mind, what they were looking for was Christian Fellowship, and how they appreciated the talk around the word of God.

The prayers that followed were very sincere and they thanked the Lord for giving them the joy of Christian fellowship.

When the number grew to fourteen, and under tropical conditions, together with the restrictions of the black-out, the men, including ourselves, felt we must get a larger room. On application to the Ship's Orderly Room, where we received the greatest help, we were allowed to use the private dining room each night from 9 to 10 pm. Our numbers still grew when we took over this room until they doubled, and when we announced a Prayer Meeting for the Saturday night, much to our joy, we had a record number…

These Meetings have been a great encouragement to all concerned, and the men have been most appreciative of what has been done for them. We have seen very appreciable changes in the spiritual life of some of these men, and it has been a great joy to have played a part in it.

Last Sunday night we announced a Gospel Testimony and the room was absolutely full, not a seat left, so some sat on the floor. This was a grand Meeting, and the Lord blessed it to at least one who said he had been a hypocrite, but now saw the Truth. We have also held hymn community singing on deck. We started this in a small way with a great deal of encouragement. It transpired on the next day or so, after we had started, that the Authorities put it in Orders for Sunday evenings. This, again, was a wonderful eye opener, hundreds of men gathered round to sing the old hymns. It was really a great joy to hear all these men singing at the close of the day that grand old hymn 'Abide with me.' It was most impressive and thank God His Word made an impression on some of their hearts.

Many an evening it has been our joy to get among the men like this, always including a reading of God's Word and a very short address. We have seen blessings abound at these open-air Meetings, and men have professed to accept the Lord Jesus Christ as their Saviour. No pressure was brought to bear on them, but simply the Lord's message given out and an invitation to all to be reconciled to God.

Two men in particular came to us afterwards and wanted to know Him whom to know is Life Eternal.[26] The Padre on board gave us encouragement by expressing surprise that men would gather together in such numbers for community hymn singing. He also said that while censoring letters, he had found from what men had said just how much this was appreciated and of what it had meant to them. So you see we have had a most happy time on this ship in the Lord's Work. The only thing lacking was suitable literature to give them, especially Testaments.

The British Flag, January / February 1943

Western Desert

The Allied forces in Egypt became the 8th Army in September 1941. Scripture Readers worked among its troops in the deserts of Egypt and Libya.

A Scripture Reader wrote that the desert 'is anything but a desirable place to dwell in; the cold, the sand storms and the debris of war make desolation more desolate'.

For several months I was attached to the 8th Army which was operating in the Western Desert and Libya and thank God for having been delivered on a number of occasions from death and serious injury with narrow escapes of

---

26 John 17:3.

being listed as 'a Prisoner of War.' On arrival at a well-known desert station in my desert car I pitched my tent and during the ensuing week was able to make many individual and collective contacts with both English and Colonial troops.

By friendly co-operation with the CofE and Non-conformists Padres openings were made for the conducting of voluntary services on gun-sites, dug-outs, and many other queer places, which were much appreciated by both officers and men. My accordion proved a great boon to the work, as hundreds of men in many places have sung to its music to the praise and glory of God. The efforts in this place were blessed by two men accepting the Lord Jesus Christ as their Saviour while others revealed their gratitude for the talks that took place, and one feels certain that the seed sown will bear fruit.

Sunday evening services were also conducted in the Wards of the Casualty Clearing Station, and one man said, 'It is a long time since I heard one of the good old Gospel songs.' Two or three days later a Christian Sergeant requested my going to the ward of which he was in charge. On arriving it was not long before a group was attracted to listen to the great truth of sin and salvation, to which intense interest and attention was given. On leaving I was followed by a man who revealed a desire to accept Christ and it transpired that the Sergeant's invitation to the ward was for the benefit of this man, who had become interested from the talk given three days previously; I had the joy of leading him to Christ, and what a change was witnessed in his life!

Sometime later I visited a certain camp and after a brief introduction we came to the subject of life and death, and

I spoke for some time. On leaving, I found a man waiting for me outside, who, through lack of fellowship felt he was losing the power to witness and was slipping back. I was able to help and encourage him, and sitting in the car together we had a time of prayer. Before I left, he expressed his resolve to carry on more firmly in the faith...

When the Battle of the Desert was resumed I felt constrained to proceed to the forward area in my car. Arriving at a place in the battle zone I had the privilege of visiting ships in the harbour and holding open-air services in the docks to which many were attracted, as we sang and played the old choruses. Being but a few miles from the front line I decided to visit the men, with the hope of contracting certain Christians whom I knew, but to my disappointment I learned that they were missing. Nevertheless, other men were got together and within the sight of descending enemy shells we sang and I spoke of the Lord's return, and one can be sure that these men will not forget hearing the Word—and singing 'Abide with me' in such strange circumstances.

The British Flag, January/February 1943

Advancing through Libya and Tunisia

Between November 1942 and May 1943, the Allied 1st Army advanced towards Tunisia from Algeria and the 8th Army from Egypt through Libya.

'Entering Tunisia'
(From *The British Flag, July-September 1943*)

Good progress is being made in the work with the advancing troops here in N Africa. My present position is with a Casualty Clearing Station in a forward area through which thousands of our troops pass. Great opportunities are presented every day and men listen to the Word with keen interest. The conditions here certainly lend themselves to the work, for, as the men lie or sit about without even a book to read, a talk is much appreciated. One evening I had the encouragement of being asked to speak to two different groups of men and the result was the conversion of a very fine type of man … He was not converted the first evening, but became so interested that he attended the Sunday evening service which was followed by a Bible Class. Then he made an appointment with me for the following evening, but in the morning he came to my bivouac before I had washed because he was so anxious to settle the matter. He has now gone back into action against a double enemy.

The British Flag, March/April 1943

Events have been moving so rapidly in the Middle East that news from our Readers is out-of-date before it reaches us. The following letter describes one of our Reader's experiences with the Eighth Army during its victorious campaign, which, together with the First Army, drove the Axis Forces out of North Africa:

Whilst still in contact with forward troops, the work continues. Many opportunities of preaching the Gospel are presented in varying circumstances.

I am keeping fit, though somewhat perplexed, owing to the uncertainty of my position as the distance from Cairo increases. At the present moment I am about 1,700 miles from the Base, with the distance rapidly increasing as one moves forward with the Army. My car broke down, and for the last 900 miles I have been begging a lift, for the most part on the back of a water lorry.

Wonderful opportunities for work are presented day by day, and many have expressed their gratitude, in various ways, for the Word they have heard.

Having represented the Association in the desert with the Eighth Army since June 1941, I have been very reluctant to leave them, despite the many difficulties I have had to contend with.

For the first thousand miles, when I had the car, and we were always on the move, the inner man was catered for by calling in at the various Field Maintenance Centres to draw rations. It was a standing joke, when those concerned learned that the unit consisted of one man! Nevertheless the usual indent was made out, and to make things easier, rations were issued to cover the period of one week, which I cooked and consumed in the mess tin with which I had been presented.

These stops on the side of the road to 'brew up' afforded many opportunities of contacting small units, which would not normally have any kind of service, so I found that the wireless set, and my dear old accordion attracted the fellows and many little groups have been thus formed, and the message of God's love in Christ has been given through the Word and music.

Travelling along a lonely road towards evening, I was looking for a site to camp and cook, when I saw a unit parked for the night with heavy lorries, so I pulled in, and the sight of this lovely painted car immediately attracted their attention. I went across and introduced myself, and seeing that I had called at the most appropriate time, when the grub stakes were going, I was invited to dine upon 'bullies' and lovely tinned potatoes, followed by tinned fruit and another mug of tea.

Following this, the wireless was installed in the cook's truck, and we listened for some time to the news and to music. I had previously requested an item informing the men that I did not know the latest songs, but could only play choruses, such as 'Love won on Calvary.' One man in the crowd asked me if I knew the hymn, 'He died of a broken heart,' and while playing this the man sang the words most beautifully, while the other men (about twenty-five in all) listened to the Gospel Message, as I used the tailboard of the truck as a platform.

Having a little engine trouble one Sunday, while it was pouring with rain, and being in rather a despondent position in the desert, I was grateful to sit inside the car (which I must say had an excellent body). I watched the rain pattering down, while the engine refused to work, in spite of the attention one normally gives when a car stops. After some time a friendly lorry driver towed me some distance, and eventually I was driven into a battery of artillery that was prepared for ground action. The mechanics put the car in order, and I asked if I might stay for the night. On being granted permission, I fixed up the wireless in one of the gun carriers and we had the pleasure of listening to some of the Church bells which were rung on that particular night to celebrate the victory of the Eighth Army. Following this item there was a speaker, who mentioned in his talks, that all were the children of God, afterwards this led me to speak of the great condition as found in John 1:12 (as many as received Him, to them gave the power to become the sons of God) which was the only means by which that glorious relationship could be formed. At the conclusion of the talk, one of the little group in this gun carrier said, 'Can we have prayer, sir?' to which I gladly responded, and before leaving, another said, 'This is a night we shall never forget.'

What will ever remain the most important part of our work is the personal contact. At the moment I am visiting men who are through a Casualty Clearing Station to which I am, for the time being attached. Much blessing is derived from the work as the definite fundamental truth of the Word of God is proclaimed, to those going in, and to those coming out of the line. Needless to say a number of Christians are met from time to time, and many happy times of fellowship, prayer, and Bible reading have been enjoyed.

In spite of instructions from Headquarters that Readers should always be smart, I think that it might be a shock to some, if they could see one of these Readers dressed in an old battledress, a hat that is much the worse for wear, with hair getting a little long, owing to the present shortage of hairdressing saloons in these parts, and a pair of captured Italian alpine boots, a bit on the large side, complete with nails.

There are moments when the ploughing of such a lonely furrow becomes vivid, especially when I think of my wife and little girls. Being the fourth year of separation, I long for the time, God willing, when I can rejoin them.

The British Flag, July/August 1943

Truly God has blessed and undertaken, and He surely will continue to do so. Never was there a greater need for the testimony that the Society bears. What an opportunity! A constantly changing population of tens of thousands of young men. I do not think that the Army of to-day differs very much really from that of the last war; profanity and obscenity are just as common whilst the fear of man is still a strong deterrent to open confession, even when conviction is very evident. It happens so often that there is 'only a step' to be taken to Jesus, but a hurried glance round at man, and alas the step is not taken, not publicly at least. Please pray for us. I have to emphasize the need of repentance when seeking to expose the sins that prevail. Only when thus aroused can men really behold with grateful love the Lamb of God. God has been very gracious, however and granted much encouragement, but how we long for greater things; oh, to see queues lining up to hear the Gospel, such as line up for the pictures, many of whom perchance may so soon pass into eternity. Please pray. E W.[27]

Ready, September/October 1943

---

27 Scripture Reader E Wigg, who served in the Middle East between 1940 and 1944.

5. Working with women of the army and air force (1942-45)

Timeline

1938-39

- Women's branches of the British armed forces were formed including the ATS (Auxiliary Territorial Service of the Army) and WAAF (Woman's Auxiliary Air Force).

1941

- December: the National Service Act (No 2) made the conscription of women legal. At first only childless widows and single women 20 to 30 years old were called up, but later the age limit was expanded to 19 to 43 (50 for First World War veterans).

By 1942, permission had been granted for the appointment of Lady Scripture Readers to work among Service women. At first, they only worked in Rest Rooms, hospitals, etc. Later, they were also given access to Barracks.

'A Restroom and Canteen'
(From a set of slides used by Scripture Readers)

We have been encouraged by the reports that have come from various centres about the work amongst the women of the ATS and WAAF. Miss D Pigott, on the completion of her first month at Honiton, realizes that it was indeed a call from God that causes her to be where she is. The Rest Room is well used by the ATS. 'Family worship' with hymn singing each evening is well attended, and the quiet chats around the fire are productive of much blessing; it can be recorded that some have expressed their acceptance of salvation.

During a recent visit to Headquarters by Mrs Donald, we heard something of what the Rest Room in Edinburgh has meant to quite a number of ATS and WAAFs as well as to Soldiers and Airmen. On one occasion, following an impressive Gospel Message from Mr Robert Laidlaw, there were several—both men and women—who professed conversion, and similar reports come from other workers.

Ready, November 1941

'ATS Dispatch Riders and traffic control'
(From a set of slides used by Scripture Readers)

The work among the ATS is in its pioneer stage, and one can only describe its beginnings. There is here a large Training Camp (1,600 girls), where recruits are received, put into uniform, vaccinated, inoculated, and generally put through an intensive training. Every Friday there is the arrival of the 'Intake,' and later on these same girls will be drafted out to their various units to take up duties with the Anti-Aircraft, or for Radio Location, or other work with the Forces.

Upon hearing from various girls that they often arrived tired and hungry, we obtained permission from the Commandant to provide tea and a bun for each girl; so each Friday afternoon several of us make ready in a hall near the Station. Soon, a batch of girls under their NCO is marched in, given refreshments and a card of invitation to the Rest Room, and is specially invited to tea on Sunday and to the informal Service following. These girls soon go off to the Camp and another group take their place. In this way we are able to be the first to give a friendly welcome, and to ensure that every girl has an invitation. The girls are most appreciative, for some are feeling very strange and nervous as to what the future holds, though others approach it all in the spirit of adventure. Older women are coming in, too, and for them it is far more difficult.

The week-ends are our busiest time, and were you able to visit us you would see the room well filled with girls; some having tea, some writing letters or reading. Then after tea one or another will choose a favourite hymn, or sing a solo, or all join in the choruses, and then listen attentively to the evening message. The numbers at these informal meetings have steadily increased until last Sunday we numbered 50. Many remark on the flowers on the tables, and how like home it all is. On my first Sunday, a Christian girl from the Camp brought with her a group of 'bright young things,' who, with a few others, gathered around the piano for hymn-singing. The humour of the situation seemed to come over them in waves: 'Look at old So-and-So singing hymns' one would exclaim, and suppressed giggling would follow. However they were strangely quiet and thoughtful as the message was given. Later we heard that the noisiest girl of all was led to Christ by her friend in the Camp.

Are these girls responsive? On the whole, yes—many are very homesick and respond to any little kindnesses shown to them—such as a piece of plaster put on a heel made sore by the new shoes, or placed on a 'vaccination arm' or a 'help-on' with the rather heavy service respirator. They are amazingly frank in their conversation (sometimes rather amusingly so) love to speak of home and loved ones, and of their Church, and especially of some soldier, now in the Middle East, or a sailor on the high seas, and the hymn 'For those in peril on the sea' is often chosen and sung with real meaning. Perhaps an older woman will speak of her children (many are married), and many another will tell of tragedy that has come into her life, wrecking her home.

The following up of these contacts made in the Rest Room is the most difficult part, and our opportunity is so short. One realises that the 'In-take' of one week-end is 'confined to barracks' the next week-end through vaccination and inoculation and the following week-end sometimes the second dose of injections. Thirty-six hours leave is granted during the last week-end for those who live near enough to take advantage of this time to go home, and then the following Wednesday, these will be the outgoing draft, posted to their various duties. One realises too, how straight and to the point the messages must be and it is our earnest prayer that God will take His Word home to the hearts of the hearers, by the power of the Holy Spirit.

One longs to be of real service to these girls, endeavouring to help them with their individual problems and leading them into vital contact with the Lord Jesus Christ. Only His power can keep them true in the time of temptation.

Surely the need is great and the difficulties are many, and one is tempted to cry 'Who is sufficient for these things?'[28] but—'Our sufficiency is of God,'[29] and we have His promise, 'He that goeth forth and weepeth, bearing precious seed, shall DOUBTLESS come again with rejoicing, bringing his sheaves with him.' (Psalm 126:6)

Miss D Pigott.

The British Flag, January/February 1942

WOMEN'S AUXILIARY

A letter from the Vice-chairman was read reporting upon a visit to the Chaplain General. The Staff Chaplain pointed out that the Churches Committee was representative of the various Churches, and that this was the reason representation had not been extended to the Association. He stated that the Chaplain General was favourably inclined to the appointment of Women Army Scripture

---

28 2 Corinthians 2:16.

29 2 Corinthians 3:5.

Readers to fields of service selected by him; such Women Readers, after nomination by the Association, would have to be approved by both the Chaplain General and by the Director of Auxiliary Territorial Service, and they would not work in uniform.

Colonel McCormack proposed and Major Clarke seconded the following resolution:–

> 'That the Council welcomed the opportunity of working amongst Service Women in Barracks under the conditions laid down by the Royal Army Chaplains' Department, and proposed to put into operation the experiment referred to on the above Minute.'

It was decided that, when the position was clarified, Mrs Bladwin (sic), Mrs Gibbon, and Mrs Pickard might be considered for appointments of an experimental nature, if the Stations occupied by them coincided with those selected by the Chaplain General.

Council Minutes, 18 May 1942

A girl, brought up in a cultured home, was found feeling lonely outside our Rest Room. She came in, was responsive to the truth, and very shortly afterwards joined our band of Christians. Did she hide her light? Was this something for Parade Service or Sunday only? No! That same evening she quietly told the girls in her hut what had happened, and the following Sunday found her at our evening service with one of her comrades. This girl came to know the Lord Jesus Christ also, and the young ATS was the means of leading seven of her squad to the Saviour, and this within the first two months of her Christian life! She was a beautiful example of the transforming power of the grace of God. Everyone liked her and week by week she found her way to the Rest Room bringing others.

One week a large intake to her Section resulted in some of the girls getting back from the city by a later bus than was permitted. The result was—'confined to barracks,' and this within a very short time of their entering Army life. Sunday was our friend's day off, and she very much wanted to go to Church, but seeing the distress of those recruits at their enforced confinement, she asked for and obtained permission to hold a little Service in her hut. There this very young Christian for the first time conducted a simple service, and you may perhaps imagine with how much trembling she uttered her first public prayer. Can we ever estimate the value of such a life? and this is only one!

There is no limit to what God can do through many such girls. May we count upon your prayers for them? Their need is the nation's need, and God has given us an amazing opportunity to take the message of the Gospel to them—'For it is the power of God unto salvation to everyone that believeth.'[30]

The British Flag, October-December 1942

…we now have 19 lady workers, including 3 lady Scripture Readers, and 1 lady worker in Canada.

Ready, March/April 1943

---

30 Romans 1:16.

'Off to their first station'
(From a set of slides used by Scripture Readers)

The first night the CO took me round some of the rooms; in one I found a Christian girl belonging to the Salvation Army. This was a great encouragement for which I thanked God. The next night when I went to the Orderly Room this Christian girl opened the door to me, and exclaimed: 'All is ready for you; there are such a lot of girls,' and she led me into the Mess Room where the girls were gathered, and I told them what I was there for. Then I tried to learn their names so as to become more friendly, and they said: 'Don't call us by our surnames, I'm Betty, or Ann, etc.' This gave a feeling of friendliness at once and I went home feeling happy and thanked God for His goodness.

It is often hard to find the girls free, however, as many of them work at different hours, some are working at night as clerks and lorry drivers, and sleep in the afternoons; but I believe God is blessing the work. Underneath the frivolous spirit there is a longing for something more. Certainly the work amongst the women and girls presents a challenge to prayer which we must face. Temptation is strong, especially to those who have left home for the first time and have not had the blessing of a Christian upbringing. It is such as these who so need to know the power of the Saviour who is able to save and to keep. A great and effectual door is open but we cannot say how long this will remain so, and the glorious opportunity of winning these girls be ours.

The British Flag, March/April 1943

Opportunities are opening up, in answer to prayer, for work amongst the women, and our Lady Workers have been in contact with members of the ATS, WAAF, WRNS, Land Girls,[31] and on one occasion one of our Workers was invited to visit a Forestry Camp.

The British Flag, September/October 1943

---

31 Land Girls were members of the Women's Land Army which was created in June 1939. Originally voluntary, conscription was introduced in December 1941. By 1944, there were over 80,000 Land Girls.

'ATS in France'
(From a set of slides used by Scripture Readers)

For many months one of our Workers was distressed at the seeming lack of response they had had to the appeal of the Gospel, but in a recent letter she tells of how they were rejoicing over answered prayer.

'Within the last fortnight,' she writes, 'We have had the joy of seeing six girls truly born again. To God be all the glory. The breakthrough for which we have been longing, seems to have really come at last in answer to prayer. We waited long, but it is better so than anything hurried or superficial. Four of the girls are ATS, two of whom have already been posted, one WAAF stationed here, and a WRNS who has left to go abroad. She had been coming to us for over a year, and had many times been convicted. I think 'going abroad' has brought her to the point.'

One Monday evening after the Blackboard Meeting one of the girls put on her outdoor clothes to go straight off, but I thought and sensed that she was miserable. I saw her to the door, but after a little word together she came back with me to a quiet place.

She said she was miserable because she didn't seem to be getting anywhere, and after what she had heard at the Blackboard Meeting, she felt she hadn't got what I had got. I told her that it was not a case of 'what' but 'Who.' It transpired that she was a Methodist, brought up in the Church and a Sunday School Teacher and we thought she was a Christian. She had all the frills and trimmings, but she hadn't got HIM.

She said she was first convicted when she saw me talking to the girls in their bedroom. She longed to talk to them too but didn't know what to say.

However, we went through verses in the Word together and she confessed that her sin had not been dealt with, Christ was not in her heart, but she was definitely seeking Him. It was a joy to bring her to the Lord and to witness the miracle of the new birth in her heart and life. She went back to her billet no longer miserable but rejoicing.

The British Flag, January/February 1944

First-hand evidence of the value of the work of the Lady Scripture Readers was provided by the testimonies of two members of the ATS. A sergeant from Nottingham said how glad she was that she had entered the Army, for there she had found the Lord. Previously she had imagined that being a Christian meant going to church on Sunday and dispensing with religion for the rest of the week. All such false notions had now been dispelled and she could not find words in which to express the joy she experienced in knowing the Saviour's continual presence. A private from Leicester spoke of her religious upbringing, in consequence of which she knew little about the fundamental truths of Christianity until in a Rest Room of the Association she had heard the Gospel and learned that Jesus Christ was the Rock to Whom she must look for salvation. Life in the Army was hard at times, but she could rejoice in it for there she had come to know the Lord.

Miss Rosemary Harris[32] said she had been amazed at the depths of depression and sin to which a sense of loneliness could take girls in the Forces. One who had subsequently been led to Christ, had travelled to a seaside town with intent to take her life. But as she gazed into the cold, dark water, thinking that in one minute all would be over, it seemed that someone was holding her back and saying, 'Don't waste your life.' She glanced round, and finding that no one was near, realised that God had spoken to her. The dread deed uncommitted, she returned to her billet, later found her way to the Rest Room, told her story, gained joy and peace in believing and has since been used to point others to Christ.

She had often been asked, said Miss Harris, how she could attempt to approach Service girls most of whom seemed so tough. She had found however, that the apparent toughness was often only a veneer to hide a broken heart, and that they were a field 'white already to harvest'.[33]

Ready, November/December 1945

---

32 Miss Harris was a Lady Scripture Reader in Yorkshire.

33 John 4:35.

6. Italy (1943-45)

Timeline

Whilst Italy surrendered in September 1943, the Allies made slow progress up Italy due to strong Axis defences, mountainous terrain and, from the summer of 1944, the redeployment of some Allied troops to France. There were over 300,000 Allied casualties during the Italian campaign.

1943

- 9-10 July: Operation Husky—the Allies invaded Sicily.
- 25 July: Mussolini (Italian leader) was arrested.
- 3 September: the Allies crossed Straits of Messina onto the Italian mainland.
- 8 September: Italy surrendered and German forces took control.
- 9 September: Operation Avalanche—the Allies landed at Salerno south of Naples.
- 12 September: Mussolini was freed by Germans.
- 1 October: the Allies captured Naples.

1944

- 15 January to 11 May: the Allies were held on the Gustav Line, a fortified zone between Naples and Rome (it included Monte Cassino).
- 22 January: Operation Shingle—the Allies landed at Anzio 30 miles south of Rome. German counterattacks held the Allies to the beachhead until 23 May.
- 4 June: the Allies captured Rome.
- 30 August to April 1945: Battles were fought around the Gothic Line, a fortified zone north of Pisa and Florence.

1945

- 2 May: German forces in Italy surrendered.

Chapter 6

After many efforts and much prayer I was able to get across to the scene of action in Europe and went first to Eboli, near Salerno. During the lull in the fighting before Cassino, I was just outside Naples. Besides open air meetings in my camp, I helped to run a Sunday afternoon Open Air Service in conjunction with some American believers in the Via Roma, Naples. Here also a meeting was commenced for the 'Breaking of Bread' to remember the Lord.

At the close of one of our open air meetings in the Camp, a man came to my tent enquiring after more help. He said that he had been listening to us and believed that we had the truth and he wished to possess this Eternal Life we had spoken of. After some conversation over the Word of God, he knelt with me and yielded to Christ. After praise and prayer I began to take his name and address and was astonished when he jokingly said 'Didn't you know, I'm bomb happy.' I had heard much about 'bomb happy'. A man whose nerve had failed him and when enemy planes came over he would run amok through the Camp causing havoc. Oftentimes it took six men to lie on him and keep him steady until the raids were over. Now here was the man! What would be the power of his new found life in Christ?

That very night, through the arrival of the large Convoy with reinforcements ready for the coming offensive, Naples experienced its heaviest raid of the war. I was lying on my camp bed as everything the AA had opened up and bombs and shrapnel began to fall around. My tent flap opened and a voice said 'Are you OK Mr B?' Cheerily assuring the enquirer that I was and inviting him in, who should it be but Bill H—'bomb happy'.

Springing out of bed, I slipped on my coat and thought now I must be ready to hold him if he runs wild. Just then some poor neurotic fellow went stumbling past the tent and to my amazement Bill went rushing out shouting 'Come in here, you don't want to be frightened, put your trust in God.' I just could not help seeing the funny side of this situation and then my spirit soared in praise to God for the delivering power of the Blessed One 'Who by death, might destroy him that had the power of death, that is, the devil, and deliver them, who through fear of death were all their lifetime subject to bondage.'[34]

Monte Cassino

On the Western side of the Italian peninsular, the German defensive line was based on the Garigliano, Rapido and Liri Rivers and Monte Cassino. The Allies made several attempts to storm Monte Cassino between 17 January and 19 May 1944, suffering about 55,000 casualties in the campaign.

Monte Cassino after the fighting

The Staff Chaplain 8th Army, the Rev John Waddington of St Peter Mancroft, Norwich, was very helpful in making

---

34 Hebrews 2:14-15.

it possible for me to get into the front line work which I had felt burdened of the Lord to do. In April 1944 Mr Bill Gough ASR, who had come all through the desert campaigns and myself joined forces and moved up into the vicinity of Cassino.

During the days before the battle opened, we visited men as they waited in their dug-outs and slit trenches. At the foot of Monte Camino[35] we came across a platoon of the Rifle Brigade enjoying some steaming hot stew which had just been brought up for them. After a cheery greeting and a little word of explanation as to who we were, Bill unslung his piano accordion and we sang duets to them. The tunes they knew but our words appealed strongly to them. To the tune of 'Carry me back to old Virginia' we sang these words: 'Carry me back to dear sweet Calvary' (contrast to Cassino). 'That's where the living waters never cease' (contrast to bloody waters of the R. Liri). 'That's where the saints sing so sweetly in God's sunshine' (contrast to the cursing and shrieks of wounded men here). 'That's where the blood makes my heart as white as snow' (contrast to the mud and blood all around).

Then we each gave a brief testimony and when I made an appeal to these fellows who knew that within a day or so they would be going forward into one of the bloodiest battles of this war, tears were evident in every eye and one after another stepped forward to shake our hands. One was so choked that one could only murmur to each: 'God bless you chum; you'll never regret your decision for Christ.' Most of these lads muttered: 'Gawd bless you Sir, you've made me feel good inside.' There were so many

---

35 Monte Camino was captured by the Allies on 3 December 1943.

men to be reached that little time could be spent with any one group.

That our witness among these men was sincerely appreciated by them and proved a real blessing may be seen by the following extract from a letter which I received from the Mother of one of these fellows. She writes: 'When we have such men as you with our boys over there, I am sure life must be worth fighting and living for with your kindness, thought and sympathy to my son.'

Pressures working near the front line

The stresses of working in forward areas (near the front line) are described in the following passage. It took a toll on Scripture Readers' physical and emotional health.

The British Army in Italy, 1944

One has often been asked what it feels like to be in the forward areas and especially in the front line. I find it hard to describe. One has a 'sense' of the atmosphere, a sort of feeling that is more emotional than mental. Either you felt it was secure to go on or not. There is a hush over the gap between the advancing army and the retreating enemy. Everything goes to earth. Every road is quite clear of traffic, except as you come across a burnt out tank still smoking, or an overturned gun with its crew lying around dead and the horses (for the Germans used many) too. Discarded helmets and webbing of the enemy lies around.

The turning of every corner is a little adventure in itself. Here and there a farmhouse burns quietly and there is no one to quench it. You hardly take your eyes off the road for a second. The enemy is a master hand at laying his deadly teller mines[36] and other abominations. When the enemy gets the slightest suspicion of any movement the hush is broken by the swish and crack of shells and the sharp staccato din of machine gun fire manifesting his nervousness. Naturally our own artillery return their fire and so the noise becomes deafening.

It was after a six-day spell like this in the vicinity of Citta di Pieve[37] that my colleague ... cracked up. We returned to Rome through which we had driven so triumphantly with the advanced elements of the 24th Guards Brigade on the day it was liberated a month or so before. There we commended each other to God and with real sorrow of heart at losing his grand fellowship.

---

36 Teller mines: German plate-shaped antitank mine.

37 Citta di Pieve is about 30 miles south west of Perugia.

With the Royal Artillery

ASR Brotherton had worked among the troops at Sheringham and Cromer on the north Norfolk coast between 1939 and 1941. This included a number of Royal Artillery (RA) regiments.

I was thrilled one day as I crossed to another sector of the line about ten miles south of Florence, to see the sign of the clover leaf. This indicated to me the presence of the 8th Indian Division. (One had to know all the signs and serial code numbers of Units to move about intelligently.) With this Division was the 53rd Field Regt RA. Many of the fellows in this Regiment had received much blessing through my ministry in Sheringham. Soon locating their number I followed the signs along devious tracks over the hills.

It was just wonderful the reception I got from these old friends as I turned into the yard of a farm and pulled up amongst a group of them doing maintenance duty on trucks. The first who looked up and saw me could hardly believe his eyes, and then yelled out to the others. As he rushed to grab my hand 'Boys, it's Mr B.' My heart was heavy as I learned of the death in action of one and another. We had a grand Service that night in the farmyard and it was fascinating to watch the expressions on the faces of fellows who had only joined the Regiment out there and did not know me, but had heard so much about me. Down at RHQ the welcome was just as warm and the Commanding Officer asked me if I would stay with the Regiment as long as I possibly could. For several weeks I held Services daily on the gun sites, often being interrupted by fire orders. The men said they would rather put up with the interruptions than be denied the blessing they derived from these informal Services.

Whilst in a Battery Command Post one morning, a message came over the field telephone from the Medical Officer asking me if I would visit with him a shell-shock case on one of the gun positions, intimating that he thought that the main need was for my ministration rather than his... Within a few minutes of this call, I met him at the rendezvous appointed and set off in his jeep. He drove, and his driver-batman sat on the metal stretcher frames at the back. We slowly picked our way along the devious tracks over the hills until we reached a path which ran right and left. Capt. M turned left but was immediately informed by his driver that he had gone wrong. Reversing and stopping, Capt. M picked up his large-scale map and said: 'confirm our position and whether we ought to turn right before we go on.'

While he was doing this I seized the opportunity for a word in season, and turning to the driver said: 'Good for you Fred, not many chaps would have spoken up so quickly and told their senior Officer that he was wrong.' Now what you have done is something like the work I am out here for, namely, to indicate which is the Right Path in life to men for 'there is a way that seemeth right unto a man but the end thereof are the ways of death',[38] and 'broad is the way that leadeth to destruction and many there be which go in thereat, because strait is the gate and narrow is the way which unto life and few there be that find it.'[39]

Capt. M had turned and listened with avid interest and immediately I had finished said: 'That's good, I've never

---

38 Proverbs 16:25.
39 Matthew 7:13-14.

heard it put over like that, what is the right way into life?' Pulling out my pocket Testament and turning to John 14:6, I passed it to him to read and aloud he read: 'Jesus said, I am the Way, the Truth and the Life, no man cometh unto the Father but by Me.' I asked: 'Is there any word there too difficult to understand?' 'Why no,' he replied, 'it is wonderfully simple and I see that the Way is a Person not a code of living or creed. Tell me, what can I do to know Him as you know Him and speak of Him?' Turning back a few pages to chapter 1, verse 12, he now read: 'but to as many as received Him, to them gave He the power to become sons of God, even to them that believe in His Name, which were born, not of blood, nor of the will of the flesh, nor of the will of man, but of God.'

I pointed out that this was the New Birth which Christ taught was so essential when He said: 'Except a man be born again he cannot see the Kingdom of God. Ye must be born again' (John 3:3,7). Whipping off his beret he said: 'I ask Jesus Christ now to come into my heart as my own personal Saviour and Lord' then turning to Fred said: 'and what about you Fred?' But alas! Fred was under no sense of need.

All the time that I spent with this Regiment afterwards, the MO and myself worked as a team at his suggestion. As he visited each position and tended to the men's physical ailments I spoke to them God's message, or as one wit put it: 'The MO gives us the pink pill and Mr B gives us the Gospill!'

Going on to visit the shell-shock case after Capt. M's decision for Christ, we had hardly stopped at our destination when we all had to throw ourselves flat as a shell from the enemy whistled over us and hit an olive tree barely ten yards away. When we looked round, it was to see the man whom we wanted running for his life down the hillside in panic. His comrades informed us that he had dug a hole in the lower slopes into which he cowered when the enemy fired. Other shells came over as I went down to him. The poor fellow was in an awful state indeed, crying and screaming with fright as he tried to claw further into the ground.

Kneeling down beside him and getting hold of him, the Lord gave me comforting and assuring words which steadied him. Within a few moments he turned and grasped my hand as I told him of the Saviour Who was waiting to come into his life, with the promise that He would never leave nor forsake him, to be in very deed 'a friend that sticketh closer than a brother'.[40] Gradually he calmed and asked me to pray for him. I commenced to pray and had just asked God to assure this lad that nothing can harm those who are in His Kingdom without His Divine will, when a shell crashed into the hillside about five feet from us, covering us with earth and throwing us into a heap. Slowly we extricated ourselves from the tangle and feeling all over realised that by a miracle of God's deliverance we had not received a scratch or a bruise.

The MO and a party of men came rushing down the hill with stretchers, as they thought, 'to carry away the pieces,' and were amazed to find us unhurt. I had experienced many wonderful escapes under fire but this seemed to transcend all.

---

40 Proverbs 18:24.

Work in Florence Prison

Scripture Readers often visited military detention barracks to speak to prisoners. Florence was near the front line between August 1944 and April 1945.

The Florence Prison was requisitioned and used as a Court Martial Centre and Detention Barracks. Following an appeal for help by the SCF (for several hours a day) I visited this gloomy, depressing hole of a place. The moment the great iron-studded door was secured behind one as you entered, a feeling of doom and disaster came over you. I never failed to feel this though I went daily for nearly four months. The Commandant was always most helpful and I wandered from one cell to another sowing the precious seed of God's Word.

Returning to my billet on Friday 12th January, 1945, ... I solicited the information that at four o'clock the next morning a firing party from that billet were under orders to take the coffin to the Prison and execute judgment upon a man sentenced to be shot. As I went to my own billet my heart was so heavy that I could not eat. Deciding to return to the Prison, I rang up the Commandant and asked if this information was correct. He assured me that it was so and also expressed the hope that I would visit the fellow and be of some help to him.

Before going across to the special block where the condemned man was, I saw the Commandant who seemed dissatisfied with this man's case. Knowing that I must not tell the man that he was due to die within a few hours I entered his cell and found him sitting between his escort finishing his supper. He glowered suspiciously at me as I entered and I knew that he was saying to himself 'Hello, who's this fellow; what does he want of me?' With heart uplifted to God for guidance I greeted all three and seated myself beside D.

'You are in a bit of a jamb and need a pal' I remarked, and then made a point of contact by discovering that he came from my native city of Birmingham. It wasn't long before I was being told in a broken, disjointed way his story of the events leading up to his being in such a dreadful predicament.

He was a driver in a REME unit stationed some ten miles south of Florence and his main job had been to bring men on Day Pass into the city each day. It was his duty to park the vehicle in an appointed place and wait until the men were due to return at nine o'clock in the evening. However, at the request of Officers from his unit he would often drive into nearby villages and try to barter tins of bully beef and biscuits for eggs and wine for the Mess.

In the centre of a village one day he sat eating his lunch, when, as was so common, a woman and her children came up to the truck asking for 'biscotti, chocolata, parre, biff' (biscuits, chocolate, bread, beef). He discovered that she had eggs to barter in the house and as she turned to enter he jumped down from his truck, still with open jack-knife lying in his hand and a packet of biscuits for the three children. Apparently the little girl, nine years of age, went to snatch the biscuits and he, teasingly, pushed her away. Unfortunately the point of the knife protruding from his hand nicked her chest causing a slight wound. Seeing the blood and knowing the fanaticism of the Italians over small things, he thought discretion the better part of valour and drove into Florence.

The next week he returned to the same spot hoping naturally to see the girl playing about and none the worse for her slight wound received so accidentally. However, to his grief and consternation the villagers gathered threateningly around him and he learned that the child had collapsed and died some hours after the incident. Two USA Military Police on patrol saw the crowd and upon investigation escorted him to the British Special Intelligence Branch in Florence and charged him with murder. D … spoke with sincerity and I was convinced he was telling me the truth.

A few questions I put revealed the fact that his soul was as dark as night concerning the things that matter most. He could never recall ever having been in a place of worship: never had he read the Bible or any portion of it, and no one had ever spoken to him of God, of Heaven, or Hell.

Spreading out my Bible between us, we read together aloud the 26th and 27th chapters of Matthew's Gospel. One could see that as we read of the Son of God being wrongfully accused and misjudged and put to a shameful death, D was deeply moved. Truly the Holy Spirit was enlightening the understanding. After explaining these and other Scriptures, D expressed a wish to receive the Lord Jesus Christ as his Saviour and thus we knelt side by side upon the concrete floor. The two soldiers on escort stood with heads bowed, faces tense and eyes strangely moist.

The glory of God filled that cell—I can never forget it. The conflict for that precious soul within those four grey walls, near at hand hundreds of men in their respective cells banging on the doors, shouting and cat-calling to one another, and outside the great big world rushing on with its madness. Tears flowed freely in that condemned cell as we rose from our knees.

That I might have something to comfort his wife and mother should the worst happen, I asked him if he would record his decision in writing, and among my few souvenirs I treasure most of all a scrap of paper containing these words; written in that condemned cell:

'Whilst under sentence of death, I wish to testify that on Friday evening after Mr B, the ASR Evangelist, had spoken to me from the Bible about the Lord Jesus Christ, I trusted Christ as my Saviour, and by God's help will follow Him all my life.' A G D … 12th Jan. 1945.

At 10 p.m. I saw the Commandant and he confirmed the story that I had heard, I then had the opportunity to read the Minutes of the Court Martial proceedings and all the evidence of the child's mother, and the doctor further confirmed the account given me. In my judgment the charge should have been at the most one of manslaughter. Being told that only a civilian could take any action in behalf of this man I pointed out to him that I was a civilian in uniform working with HM Forces Chaplains Dept. Together we put in a strong appeal which I signed and the Commandant immediately despatched to the appropriate authority at HQ. It was now midnight, the appeal was accepted, which resulted in a stay of execution.

Daily my visitation went on with Bible Study for D on his own and for a group of others who had come to decision for Christ in a small room placed at my disposal. After many weeks I was greeted with cheers by the whole of the Prison Staff, including the RSM, and I learned that the appeal for D had been upheld. The Commandant kindly waited for me that we might take the news together to D. The sentence was commuted to penal servitude for life and he was brought to England to serve in better conditions.

7. North West Europe (1944-45)

Timeline

In June and July 1944, the Allies established a strong presence in Normandy. This was followed by a rapid advance, with almost the whole of France and Belgium liberated by the beginning of September. Axis defences, long Allied supply lines and poor weather then slowed the Allies advance until March 1945. Meanwhile, the USSR was advancing against Germany from the east and south east.

1944

- 6 June: Operation Overlord (D-Day)—the Allies landed in Normandy, France
- 25 July: Operation Cobra—the Allies broke the Axis front line in Normandy, starting more rapid advance.
- 15 August: Operation Dragoon—the Allies landed in Southern France
- 25 August: Paris was liberated.
- 3 September: Brussels was liberated.
- 17-25 September: Operation Market Garden—the Allies liberated Southern Netherlands but failed to cross the Rhine at Arnhem.
- 16-25 December: Axis counterattacked in the Ardennes (Battle of the Bulge)—they were held by the Allies before they could reach the River Meuse.

1945

- 7 March: Allies crossed the Rhine at Remagen.
- 30 April: Hitler committed suicide in Berlin.
- 7 May: German forces surrendered.
- 8 May: VE (Victory Europe) Day.

Preparing to send Scripture Readers to France

SASRA prepared to send Scripture Readers to Normandy as soon as possible after 'D-Day' (6 June). Fighting in Normandy continued until mid August 1944.

Scripture Readers 'Ready for the Second Front'
(From *The British Flag, October 1944*)

EUROPEAN FRONT

Progress reported. It was hoped that, if the present arrangements were put into effect, Mr Laidlaw and eight Readers would be in Normandy before the end of the month. Mr Taylor and Mr Davies would be retained to take over two cars, a Hudson for Mr Laidlaw (which had been obtained at a cost of £200) and a Hillman kindly given by Mrs Allen, which would not be ready until after the 7th August. The arrangements for pay, postings, petrol and feeding were reported, the latter at a cost of 1/- per head per day, which would be deducted from the Readers' pay at Headquarters. The HGS reported how helpful the Staff Chaplain at 21 AG CVWW Committee had been in formulating plans and putting them into effect.

Council Minutes, 12 July 1944

Our friends and supporters will be grateful to know, that we are sending ten of our Scripture Readers to accompany the Invasion Troops as soon as the Authorities are able to make the necessary arrangements. These will be under the superintendence of Mr Robert Laidlaw, who for the past five years nearly, has rendered the Association such valuable service as one of the Field Directors. So that friends may be able to follow the Readers by name they pray for them, they are: G Barton, A Ball, W Davies, E Farwell, C Main, R J Samson, W G Taylor, J N Watkins, W Watson, H G Young.

Ready, July/August 1944

Working with Invasion Troops

Scripture Readers worked among those preparing to go to Normandy (about 83,000 men were landed in the British/Canadian sector on 'D-Day') and those returning wounded or as prisoners of war.

'Onto the beaches D-Day'
(From a set of slides used by Scripture Readers)

June has been a happy month here evangelizing the 'Invasion Troops.' It has been a solemn thought to think that many of these men might hear their last Gospel message from my lips before going into action. I am sure the Holy Spirit has accompanied the message given.

As the time drew near to D Day the men were 'keyed up' to go overseas; some played cards to hide their feelings, others were truly solemnized.

In the Barracks I addressed about thirty in one room—a so-called atheist opposed me, but the Lord gave me grace to answer him. Two of the men desired to speak to me privately, one had led an immoral life and was really convicted. I was able to point him to the Saviour and he there and then found peace. I prayed with him and then turned to the other man, younger and of a different type, but also needing salvation. He, too, entered into rest by faith in Christ.

In a Pioneer Company I found three men in a top attic, and we had an impromptu Gospel meeting. At the close all three knelt and prayed with me accepting Christ. I called again with Testaments, and shall keep an eye on them so long as they are here.

This is only one of the many letters received from our Readers, whose experiences have been very similar, amongst those men who are now on the other side of the channel.

Now the wounded are being brought back and our Readers are having busy times in the hospitals getting into contact with them.

Wonderful opportunities are presenting themselves as many of these soldiers and airmen have been softened by their experiences and are ready to listen to the Gospel message.

'I am very happy to report times of blessing,' writes another of our Readers. 'I have been working amongst the men back from the Normandy battle front. Both officers and men have given me a very vivid description of what faith in God means in the thick of the battle; many made the great decision on the field. The good seed sown in the days of preparation has brought forth fruit now, but in many cases it was seed sown in tears: "He that goeth forth and weepeth, bearing precious seed, shall doubtless come again with rejoicing bringing his sheaves with him." Psalm 126:6.'

From 1939 to 1944 the message amongst these men has been faithfully proclaimed and His Word has not returned unto Him void.[41]

'This month has been a month of new experiences for me,' writes another Reader, 'it has fallen to my lot to visit German prisoners of war from Normandy. I could not speak German, but one or two of them could speak English so they passed on what I had to say to the others. They had no knowledge of the Bible. One young German asked me who wrote it, when I explained that it was written by inspired men of God, he said, "Are any of them German?" What a problem for us after this war.'

When on a visit to one of the wards, a soldier reading the Regimental News said: 'There is nothing but killed, wounded and missing in this Gazette.' It was in fact the Chronicle. I said, 'There is much better news in my Regimental Chronicle.' He said, 'What is it?' I pointed to John 1:29, 'Behold the Lamb of God, which taketh away the sin of the world,' and Romans 5:8, 'While we were yet sinners Christ died for us.' He said, 'That is the best news I've heard, your Regimental Chronicle is indeed the best Book in the World.' I said, 'Do you believe it?' 'Yes, sir, I

---

41 Isaiah 55:11.

do, and from to-day I will read it every day.' He had only just returned from Normandy.

I have had a busy time since the second front opened; on one visit I was able to make contact with Germans, French, Italians, Indians, Czechs and our own boys, I pray that God will guide me in this strange experience.

'For by one Spirit are we all baptized into one body, whether we be Jews or Gentiles, whether we be bond or free.' 1 Corinthians 12:13.

In one war hospital a badly wounded Corporal fixed his gaze intently on me and said, 'Go on, sir, I am deeply interested, you are telling me just what I want to hear.' He told me that on the eve of battle the Commanding Officer addressed the Battalion on the work of the morrow, and then intimated that the Padre would hold a service to celebrate Communion and all were invited to remain for it. Only eight men, including my friend, waited for it. This had so shocked the corporal that he determined to get right with God at his first opportunity. Through wounds and travail, battle and peril this was his first opportunity. It was easy to lead him to the Lord, and yet on the other hand difficult, for he feebly clung to his poor shreds of self-righteousness.

He was so thankful for faithful dealing and seemed to see clearly at last.

One thing is very noticeable about these overseas contacts and that is the absence of any desire to contradict what one says and the ready admission by one and all to the fact that the Gospel of Salvation is the only solution to the problem of men's present needs.

I was led to speak to a Private just back from Normandy and said that I had come to tell him of One Who had laid down His life for him. He immediately sat upright and enquired: 'Was it the Sergeant Major?' 'No,' I replied, 'someone far more vital than the Sergeant Major.' It appeared that he was hit and left lying out in the open, some of his comrades had tried to reach him, but had failed. However, the Sergeant Major managed to get to him and had promised to come back, but had not done so, and the lad thought he must have been hit and probably killed. Eventually he was brought in by others. He gladly heard the Gospel message.

The British Flag, September/October 1944

Scripture Readers working in Normandy

The Scripture Readers in Normandy worked among the troops landing and preparing to move further inland. The Mulberry Harbour in Normandy was a key Allied port until Antwerp (Belgium) started to be used in late November 1944.

From the summer of 1944, Scripture Readers wearing battledress wore a distinctive flash (blue on a red ground for the Army or pale blue on a dark blue ground for the RAF).

Letters are beginning to come in from our team of Readers under the superintendence of Mr Laidlaw who are now working with our troops in Normandy. One and all speak gratefully and enthusiastically of the wonderful welcome they received from both Officers and Chaplains.

Mr Laidlaw writes:

The Lord has certainly sent His angel before us preparing the way... On the ship the Lord gave us an earnest of blessing to follow; Reader —— contacted a young fellow on deck and brought him down to the Central Cabin we had been given, and together we led him to Christ.

On arriving in Normandy Mr Laidlaw, describing their reception, says: 'I haven't met one snag, so far everyone has helped in every possible way while the Chaplains Dept. has been simply wonderful.'

A Reader writes:

The Padre here introduced me to Capt. —— and from then onwards kindnesses have just been heaped upon me by all in authority in this camp. A small marquee tent has been pitched for me, the men leaving to-day are strolling in here to examine my literature on the table, make a selection and have a chat.

The literature I brought with me from Headquarters is disappearing rapidly … you can't send me too much or too frequently. The capacity of this camp is 3,500 men at a time, and they are coming and going every day. Two Canadians have just been in and have selected 'The Reason Why' and one of Arthur Mercer's booklets. We had a chat together and as we talked the older man reached for my Bible with the remark, 'You don't mind if I refresh my memory a bit?' I suggested he should read his portion to his friend and me, and with much feeling he read the twenty-third Psalm. Then we spoke of the Saviour Whose presence in our lives makes this psalm a precious reality. This is a good site as the men see the tent on arrival and can make it the last call before leaving. During their stay here I shall have opportunities of visiting them in their tents as the Lord guides me and of having meetings for them in this tent.

The British Flag, September/October 1944

Mr H G Young, told of experiences during a year with Field-Marshal Montgomery's Army Group of the BLA. In August 1944, he landed with a party on the Normandy beaches before the ports were in operation.

At a seaside resort, a small hotel, without windows or electric light and having only half a roof, provided reading and writing rooms for the men. Here, for so long as he remained, he conducted Sunday evening services. In the course of that year there were those with whom he made but a single contact, with what results it was impossible to tell. Such an occasion was a Sunday morning when 200 men who were to leave the next day for an unknown destination, and had heard that he was preaching at a small church, gained permission to attend the service. Seating accommodation was sufficient for only half their number, but they managed to pack themselves in, and they listened to the Gospel for forty minutes.

Ready, November/December 1945

Belgium

Belgium was liberated in September 1944. The front line then remained fairly static until March 1945, allowing the Scripture Readers to catch up with the British Army.

Mr Robert Laidlaw gave a descriptive account of his two months in Normandy and Belgium with our Scripture Readers.

On their first arrival it seemed as though there were going to be great opportunities for personal evangelism amongst the troops, but owing to the unparalleled successes of the BLA, which resulted in the British Army being kept continually on the move, our Readers found themselves without substantial numbers. Latterly, however, since arriving in Belgium, it is thought that things might be more static, for a while at least, and he and the Readers were looking forward to making full use of the Halls of The Belgian Gospel Mission, which had been placed at their disposal by the Director, Dr Vansteenberghe.

Ready, November/December 1944

Robert Laidlaw

'Robert A Laidlaw'
(From *Ready, January-February 1945*)

Robert Laidlaw (1885-1971) was a New Zealand businessman who founded the Farmers Trading Company. He was a Christian writer and philanthropist, most famous for writing 'The Reason Why' an evangelistic tract first published in 1913. It was used by SASRA during the war, is still in print, and has been translated into over 30 different languages. His work with SASRA is summarised below. He was awarded an MBE in the 1946 New Years Honours for his work as 'Superintendent of Scripture Readers with the British Army of the Rhine.'

At the outbreak of war, there walked into Headquarters a gentleman from New Zealand saying that he had been on his knees the day before to enquire of God His will—whether to return with his wife and family to their home in New Zealand (whence they had come on holiday) or to say good-bye to them as they returned while he remained to work for Him amongst the men of His Majesty's Forces. 'The latter,' said Mr Robert Laidlaw, 'was the decision arrived at, and I have come to enquire if there is a sphere of service for me in connection with the ASR&SACA.'

In John 1:6 we read: 'There was a man sent from God'; and, as the Council review the past five and-a-half years' ministry of Mr Laidlaw as Joint Hon. Field Director with Mr Montague Goodman, to which they were pleased to appoint him, it is only to confirm what they believed at the time of his appointment—that he was also 'a man sent from God.'

Space does not permit anything like an adequate record of what our friend accomplished during these years that he laboured amongst us but the Council does wish to place on record their deep sense of gratitude to him for his wise counsel and unstinted services, all of which were rendered in an entirely honorary capacity.

When the BEF went to France, it was thought that an opportunity was presenting itself for a work of intensive evangelism similar to that which the Association engaged in during the Great War, 1914-18. With this in view, to supplement the work of the twelve Scripture Readers. Mr Laidlaw and his colleague crossed over to the Continent. There they opened up two Rest Rooms to start with, and carried out negotiations for the erecting of a mobile Hut presented by friends in Ulster and to be known as the 'Ulster Hut,' which would accompany the troops in the more forward areas where such amenities are not usually to be found.

The collapse of France, however, brought everything to a close and, on their return to England, they commenced at once to busy themselves in the establishing of Rest Rooms up and down the Country where there were large concentrations of Service men and women. Once these were established, Mr Laidlaw set himself to the ministry of the Word in these Rest Rooms, visiting them from time to time, not only to preach the Gospel, but also to encourage the workers.

His ministry was a very fruitful one, in Rest Rooms as well as in other places of worship to which he was invited.

Shortly after 'D' Day, when the Council was looking to God for someone to superintend their team of ten Readers, who were under orders to proceed to Normandy, Mr Laidlaw volunteered in spite of his having already intimated that he was negotiating for a passage to return to New Zealand. The Council were pleased to accept this further offer and by the time the Readers were due to leave for Normandy he had gathered together his equipment and was to accompany them. After some months during which much of a pioneering nature had to be accomplished, the work had become established, when an urgent business call came, necessitating Mr Laidlaw's immediate return to New Zealand.[42] Very reluctantly, he submitted to the necessity of laying down the work which he had come to

---

42 In his autobiography 'The story of the reason why' Mr Laidlaw refers to receiving a letter from a friend telling him that his wife was feeling the strain of his absence.

love so well, and the Council have been indeed sorry to have to say good-bye to such a faithful colleague.

Ready, January/February 1945

Germany

The Allies crossed the Rhine in March 1945 (the Americans at Remagen on 7 March and the British at Wesel on 23 March). Whilst the German leadership ordered that a desert should be created in the Allies' path, many Germans surrendered.

As we go to press the news of the victorious and rapid advance of our troops over the Rhine and into Germany gives us reasonable hope of an early cessation of hostilities in Europe. When that time arrives the Association will be faced with an unparalleled opportunity. The reaction from the strain of fighting will mean that our men will be beset with many temptations. The Scripture Readers work is never finished—there is no cessation of hostilities in the war against the world, the flesh and the Devil. They need our prayers and all the help we can give them.

The British Flag, March/April 1945

Probably you will have guessed by now that we are in the land of the 'white flags'.

It appears that not everyone wishes to flee from us as some expected, nor are they being shot, as the German radio gave them to understand they would be. Few of them are beginning to realise now what lies they have been fed upon, and here we see proof of what sort of a show the devil can put up when given a free hand. How the folk blame something or somebody, apart from the right one!

What a likeness we have in principle to the soul of one who rejects the claims of Christ and accepts anything or nothing. Then follows the blaming of someone other than the right one—SELF.

I have a few booklets and Gospels in their language, and so occasionally slip one in here and there, as the Lord leads; so please pray that these small contributions to the 'NEW ORDER' may bear fruit unto Eternal Life in Christ Jesus.

Ready, May/June 1945

Occupied Germany

'Mr Davies at ASR&SACA HQ Bad Zalzuflen 21st Army Group HQ'
(From *The British Flag, October-December 1945*)

'Last Saturday I managed to get a cafe "The Laterne" situated under a public house and near GHQ, rather a central position in the compound, it holds about 50 persons. We opened up on Sunday evening with 25 to 30 men and girls present.'

'Berlin Branch'
(From a set of slides used by Scripture Readers)
At the end of the war, Austria, Germany, Berlin and Vienna were each divided into American, British, French and Soviet (USSR) occupation zones.

You will be glad to hear how your prayers are being answered in regard to the work in Berlin. The ASR and S&ACA Flat has been nicely furnished, the piano, a good one, was brought in a few days ago, a blackboard has been supplied, also Hymn Books. The Notice and Texts in the windows will help members to locate the Flat. There is a placard from SCM 'Have you read your Bible to-day?' and a text 'He that heareth my word, and believeth on him that sent me, hath Everlasting Life,'[43] is being noticed and read by many of our men. I often notice Germans reading it too.

---

43 John 5:24.

So far since the place was opened we have had a meeting every night for Bible study and prayer and we praise the Lord for one man deciding for Christ Jesus the first night it was opened. A few days before, this man was reading letters to me that he had received from his mother during the war, especially pointing out to me thoughts of God that she had written; his mother exhorting him so often to put his trust in God.

The first full member to call was Dr —— who decided for the Lord at Normandy. He was followed by many other members who are bearing a bright witness.

Ten were present at our BB Meeting on Friday, and it was a helpful and blessed time of fellowship. Each one has promised to come with prepared slips next week. I feel sure, with much prayer and the co-operation of the members, great things for the Lord will be done. The Chaplain is kindly having BB Slips[44] and invitation cards printed for me. The COs of units have been very nice and glad to hear of the work of the Association being done here.

I accompanied the Chaplain to Spandau where we visited the General Hospital and saw the building that is to be used as Church House. I mentioned to the Chaplain the possibility of another Reader commencing work in Spandau and he said, 'there would be accommodation here.'

The British Flag, November/December 1945

We arrived at a place called Gluckstadt, about thirty miles from Hamburg. This is a really first class hospital, meant

---

44 BB (Black Board) slips: each day members recorded a verse from their daily readings on the slip. These were shared at weekly meetings. For each day, the verse with the largest number of votes was recorded on a blackboard.

for German officers, and the accommodation is good. At present there are about two hundred convalescents.

You will be pleased to hear we have had some very encouraging times, especially at our Bible Classes held every night. Tpr ——— who became an associate member a fortnight ago is growing strong in the faith. It is a great joy to have Gnr ——— with us, he is an old Christian, witnessing for the Lord, and is a great help here, he is sending an application for full membership to you soon. Also we have with us Pte ———, who is a keen Christian, he too, is sending an application for full membership. I am enclosing an application for full membership for Pte ———.

The meetings held in the wards of the General Hospital, and the Community singing in the Canteen on Sundays at Celle, were great opportunities for the Gospel message. A Canadian LAC whom I met in the General Hospital, said he often read the New Testament but there was quite a lot he could not understand. I was led to give him 'The Way of Salvation.' A few days after he came to the Convalescent Depot and attended our Bible Classes and during one of these meetings he said much doubt and fear had been removed, and expressed his desire to follow the Lord.

Just as I was leaving a ward, a man asked me for a Testament and said the one he had was lost when in battle and he wished to read it through. I gave him a Testament, also, 'How to live the Christian life' and when he read 'The first essential step in the Christian life is to be "born again"' John 3:7. He wished to know more about being born again, and, through the Word of God, I had the joy of leading him to the Lord. When asked when he was going to receive Christ Jesus as Saviour? he said 'straightway.' The Chaplain left us a few days ago very hurriedly, he left a note thanking me for my loyal co-operation during these six months. Last Sunday the OC gave me permission to take the morning Service, a good number were present to hear the Gospel message.

The British Flag, November/December 1945

8. India and the Far East (1941-45)

Timeline

Between December 1941 and May 1942, the Japanese captured most of south east Asia. British losses included Hong Kong, Malaya, Singapore and Burma (Myanmar). Over the next 2 years the Allies in India learned how to fight in jungles and to supply troops by air before recapturing Burma in 1945.

1941

- 7 December: the Japanese attacked the United States fleet at Pearl Harbor.
- 8-26 December: the Japanese captured Hong Kong.

1942

- 15 February: the Allied forces in Singapore surrendered to the Japanese. There were about 138,000 Allied prisoners of war.
- 8 March: the Japanese captured Rangoon, Burma (Myanmar).
- May: Allied forces withdrew from Burma into India.
- 3-7 June: Battle of Midway—the Japanese fleet was defeated by the United States.

1944

- 7 March – 18 July: Japanese attacks on Imphal and Kohima, India were defeated by the Allies.

1945

- 3 May: Allied forces recaptured Rangoon, Burma.
- 9 August: the USSR declared war on Japan.
- 15 August: VJ (Victory Japan) Day—when the initial announcement of Japan's surrender was made.
- 2 September: Japan's surrender document was signed on USS Missouri in Tokyo Bay.

Scripture Readers in India

In January 1941 there were 5 Scripture Readers in India. Pre-war, over a third of the British Army was stationed in India, particularly in the unsettled north west border region. This was reflected in the locations of Scripture Readers which included Lahore, Peshawar and Rawalpindi, which are now in northern Pakistan (India and Pakistan were partitioned in 1947).

The following is an account of the work in India in 1939.

The Readers in India seldom find themselves stationed at one place. They usually have a district in which are several stations which they must visit. These stations are reached by various means, sometimes train, motor car, tonga[45] and bicycle are used. One must remember that travelling in India is vastly different to that in most parts of Britain. Fast, very comfortable trains and buses, destinations easily and quickly reached are found in Britain, here, the reverse is the case. When travelling by road (which is normally quickest and most convenient) one is advised to be clear of certain areas before dusk, as all natives in this part are not friendly. Because of this, and other inconveniences of travelling, and in order that the men may be visited in the evening, one is often compelled to stay overnight at the Outstations. This means packing up one's bedding, and other necessaries, and taking them with you, (this is the general rule in India). In this district suitable accommodation is scarce, sometimes the Padre kindly puts one up, if he is there, sometimes another Christian friend, and sometimes one shares the kind hospitality of an NCO in a corner of his bunk.

---

45 Tonga: a light 2-wheeled vehicle for two or four persons drawn by one horse and common in India.

A Reader's day is a long one, and true, he is often tired in it, but never of it, and by God's enabling Grace, triumphs and rejoices daily. To him his work is not just something he is paid for, which must be done, but rather he is a willing instrument in the hands of his Master, the Lord Jesus Christ. The Reader is an early riser, often before the troop Reveille, in order that he may have his quiet time alone with God in prayer and in reading His Word, before the 'Sweeper' arrives. Then comes breakfast, for he must eat, for it is said if one neglects to feed the inner man in this country especially, he will never see 'Blighty'[46] again, and surely that is the hope of most Britishers.

After breakfast, he tackles his never ending correspondence, part of which consists of writing letters to Christians in other stations to which the Reader can only pay one visit a month. Part of the day must be spent in studying God's Word, for daily he is confronted with many a hard question as he visits hospitals and barrack rooms. The afternoon and evening are spent in visiting the hospitals and barrack rooms. Often 'Lights Out' (10.15 pm) has sounded while one has sought to make known the full Gospel of God, our Heavenly Father, then back to one's own billet; a cup of cocoa, or Ovaltine and a biscuit; and a summarising of the events of the day, for future record purposes. Then to commit all things to Him who has guided, directed and controlled by His Spirit throughout the day, praising and thanking Him for the privilege which is ours, for sustaining grace and victory, ever being reminded of our responsibility as co-workers together with Him; thus the day ends.

---

46 Blighty was a soldier's name for Britain or home.

Sometimes the Reader finds his hands full in organising a Rally. This means much travelling here and there at each Station, interviewing those in authority at Military Headquarters, obtaining permission for this and that, and in all we seek to co-operate with the Padres.

The British Flag, October 1939

Singapore

Singapore was Britain's key naval and military base in the Far East. Tension with Japan had been increasing—in July 1941, following the Japanese occupation of southern Indo-China (Cambodia and southern Vietnam), all Japanese assets in the USA had been frozen.

Prayer is also requested for Singapore. Last autumn we sent Mr Sandy out as Scripture Reader, but shortly after his arrival he was invited by the Authorities to become Welfare Officer for the Command, which he has accepted, and in consequence has resigned the office of Scripture Reader.[47]

Ready, September 1941

Japanese capture of Hong Kong and Singapore

Hong Kong had surrendered to the Japanese on 26 December 1941 (about 12,000 Allied troops were captured) and Singapore on 15 February 1942 (about 138,000 Allied troops were captured). About 27 per cent of Western Allied prisoners died in Japanese captivity.

---

47 In October 1941, ASR R F C Westlake was assigned to take up the work in Singapore. He was unable to do so due to the war with Japan and instead served in Ceylon (Sri Lanka) between 1943 and 1944.

Ever since the Japanese entered the war our minds have, naturally, been turned in the direction of the Far East, where numbers of our Members are serving now that Hong Kong and Singapore are in the hands of the enemy. We cannot but wonder how our brethren are faring. Some months must elapse before we can expect to receive any definite news, but this will not prevent us from being constantly in prayer on their behalf.

Ready, March/April 1942

Retreat from Burma (Myanmar)

The Allies attempted to defend Burma but with little air or artillery support they had to retreat into India, abandoning most of their transport and heavy equipment.

Captain T T S Cooke, R. Signals, who has just returned from Burma writes:–

God's Fire in Burma

Daniel 3:25.

Below are a few of the experiences and lessons learnt by a 'believer' whilst in Burma recently.

When well 'dug in' in India, I suddenly received orders to proceed overseas. It came as rather a shock. My God soon quieted my soul with Psalm 27:3–4. We soon set out for a port, and 'He' further assured me with Psalm 77:19–20. I realised then doubly 'His Presence' was going with me.

We were soon at sea, and passed the wreckage of 2 ships which had been sunk a day or two before. 'He' quieted all doubts with Habakkuk 3:16. Later, (unknown to us till we landed) we heard that five torpedoes had missed us the last night at sea. In assurance of deliverance the Lord gave me Psalm 78:52-53.

We landed amid air warnings, and were soon to have plenty of them. How comforting to turn to His WORD, and repeatedly get 'His' assurance of being at hand. One day when bombers and fighters were high up having a scrap, He gave me Psalm 20:7-8.

Early on we experienced the weariness of night raids. The lack of fellowship cast one more on the Lord. The first service one was able to attend refreshed one no end by being greeted with the hymn 'My Jesus; I love Thee, I know Thou art mine,' after which the true gospel was preached.

Later, one had to learn to go long times without fellowship or services, and rely on the Lord and His WORD alone for strength. 2 Corinthians 11:26-27 became very real to me, but how true verse 30, and that 'His Strength may be made perfect in weakness.' [48]

We had many deliverances. Four in particular were remarkable. One, an accident to a vehicle, delayed us so that we arrived after a certain place had been severely bombed, whereas we should have been in the midst of it. Another time we were delayed by the officer leading the Convoy halting for no reason, except he felt he had to, so he told me, outside a small town. Just then a severe dose of bombs fell on the road in the middle of the town from a high level attack, so we were preserved. The third was again a delay preventing my arriving in the midst of severe bombing, and the fourth, preservation when drove through a raging furnace of flame, when the oil wells were being blown up.

Casualties in my unit were 2% only, very light, compared with the risks we ran, 'But the Almighty cast

---

48 2 Corinthians 12:9.

His Shadow'[49] continually over the men as well, some 4 or 5 being 'believers' too.

On two occasions, when in need of rations and expecting more, a Dump was opened up unexpectedly where and when we needed it; in one case it was still arriving.

Our greatest deliverance was fulfilled in 'His' promise to me in Jeremiah 45:5, and the latter half some ten days before it occurred, and when the storm clouds looked very black.

This was literally fulfilled, and not only for oneself, when one reached India safely with one's life and weapons, but nothing else.

After such deliverances, it seemed reasonable to expect a time of rest, and release from trial, but no—severe sickness got hold of me. The Lord's fire became 7 times hotter, but the fourth person still had the likeness of the Son of Man, Daniel 3:17. He is still present, and assures me of His will and purpose in giving me successively 2 Corinthians 12:9, John 11:4, and my part to play in 1 Corinthians 6:20.

I have been taught of my Father some definite lessons:–

(a) 'He' is able to deliver—nothing, no occasion is too hard.

(b) 'He' expects me to seek in Him and His WORD companionship in loneliness.

(c) 'He' expects me to witness continually to 'His' Salvation, and will give the power to do so.

(d) The uselessness of material possessions. Our Inheritance is in Heaven.

---

49 Psalm 91:1 says that 'He that dwelleth in the secret place of the most High shall abide under the shadow of the Almighty.'

(e) God is Jehovah-Jireh,[50] and can provide our every need, even if man cannot see its possibility, Philippians 4:19.

(f) 'Tribulation worketh patience, and patience worketh hope, and hope maketh not ashamed.'[51] It all serves to increase one's faith in Him—'Have the faith of God.'

(g) There is a 'Valley of the Shadow of Death',[52] but there is Light where there are shadows. One can walk through a shadow to the sunlight beyond—no shadow can hurt you. The rod God gave Moses turned into a serpent, but it also ate up those of the Egyptian magicians.[53] That same rod was used to pave the way across the Red Sea, and close the waters over the chariots of Pharaoh.[54]

Oh my Soul … Hope thou in God. Psalm 42:11, Daniel 3:17, Daniel 3:25.

Hope thou in God. Psalm 42:11.

India Reader Reports, July 1942

Scripture Readers' work in India

The following are examples of Scripture Readers' work in India. This was in hospitals and rest areas hundreds of miles behind the front line.

Bangalore.[55] Praise God for the many encouragements in His service here as a Scripture Reader. The opportunities are tremendous. The time is short. The holiday home for

---

50 Jehovah-Jireh means 'the Lord provides' (Genesis 22:14)

51 Romans 5:3-5.

52 Psalm 23:4.

53 Exodus 7:10-12.

54 Exodus 14:16.

55 Bangalore is in southern India.

men of the Forces has been filled and our visits to this camp weekly have meant the distribution of from 100-200 Gospels, and six or more New Testaments as well as large numbers of Tracts. Many have accepted invitations to Gospel meetings; and have thus contacted other believers and enjoyed Christian fellowship.

Hospitals. The Wards are visited systematically and large numbers of Gospels, Tracts and New Testaments are distributed. Many a precious contact is made, and Christian lads are encouraged by these Visits. One lad accepting a Gospel of St John, said 'I could have done with this on the Naga Hills.'[56] Another produced a copy of a New Testament which had been dropped from a plane, as it dropped supplies to a camp in Burma.

Through a kind friend I was able to purchase £3-6-0 worth of the fine edition SGM Bible, and some of the Christian lads have been overjoyed with these gifts. An order for a similar amount is now on its way to England.

Open-Air. The services conducted in the open-air every Saturday evening by service men under the auspices of the SACA continues to be a bright feature of aggressive Christian work in our midst. I was told the other week that someone remarked in mockery, that we were 'a set of glorious fools.' Yes, praise God, 'Fools for Christ's sake.'[57] Whose fool are you?

We have recently bade farewell to our young brother Graham Davies of the RAF—who was brought to the Lord while in hospital. He has borne a wonderful testimony to

---

56 The Naga Hills are part of the forested mountain barrier between India and Burma (Myanmar).

57 1 Corinthians 4:10.

the saving Grace and Power of his Lord and Saviour Jesus Christ, and took keen interest in the open-air meetings. It was a real delight to watch him on the roadside moving amongst Officers and men distributing the Word of God. The Lord richly bless him in his new station. Truly a trophy of his matchless Grace.

W A Beer. Acting SR.

Bombay.[58] Camps and Hospital. During our regular visits many men have been contacted in their own billets during the past month and much literature has been distributed. Everywhere I have had a good reception and many fruitful conversations have taken place. Again I have had the privilege of contacting men just arriving from the UK. Through the generosity of the US Army Chaplain about 400 New Testaments were given to these men and the Gospel was also presented to them by word of mouth. May God bless His own Word to these young men.

Rest Room. As a result of the visiting many now have been seen at the Rest Room. The meetings held in the Room are well attended and the Lord is blessing us. Several have decided for Christ. Our open-air witness has also been mightily used of God to bring men to know the Lord Jesus Christ as Saviour.

Geo. Whyte. SR.

India Reader Reports, November 1944

---

58 Bombay is now Mumbai.

Return to Burma

Burma (Myanmar) was recaptured between January and May 1945.

The British Army in Burma, 1945

It was strange to find one's feet on board a Troopship again, and although the journey was short, in the opinion of many it was in the wrong direction,[59] yet one found opportunity for service, and the Lord blessed the Word and added souls to His Church.

Landing in torrential rain, one prayed God would pour upon us in this new sphere showers of blessing.

---

59 Troops were looking forward to going home (west) rather than to Burma (east).

I was soon to find out that I was not the first Christian to arrive in Burma, in a few days I had met at least twenty others and since then many more, both Officers and men.

There are at least eight meetings weekly for Prayer and Bible study. These are held in various places. On Friday at 7pm we meet in the Salvation Army Club where we have a united meeting for all who are within reasonable distance. Last week we numbered over 30, almost half of them being Officers.

On Sunday there is a Team Gospel Service held in the YMCA which is well attended.

Soon we hope to add to our activities, particularly along the line of organisation.

All who love the Lord and find themselves in or near here are invited to join us in raising up out of these ruins a structure that will stand for Eternity.

T J Weaver. SR.

Ready, August 1945

9. Victory and Rebuilding (1945)

Timeline

1945

- 8 May: VE (Victory Europe) Day.
- 15 August: VJ (Victory Japan) Day.

VE Day celebrations at Caterham Primary School
(Used with permission of the Surrey History Centre)

VE Day in a Rest Room

The end of the war in Europe was celebrated throughout Britain. The following is an example from a SASRA Rest Room.

'Harrogate VE Day celebration'
(From a set of slides used by Scripture Readers)

VE-DAY found us prepared—The Union Jack fluttered from our top window—Flags of our Allies stretched across the front window, and the stairway. Over the front door hung a tin hat full of flowers, raising a smile from all passing under.

Each table had fresh beech twigs and leaves with red, white and blue bows, which have drawn endless remarks from the girls.

Our Thoughts for the week have been:

'Thanks be to God who giveth us the victory through our Lord Jesus Christ.'[60]

'The Lord wrought a great Victory[61] and He hath Triumphed Gloriously.'[62]

The Canteen was packed for the morning service—we kept open for Mr Churchill's speech at 3 pm then handed tea and biscuits round, and then listened to the wireless service which followed. We shall never forget the crowds in the evening during the King's speech. Every table and all up the stairs was filled: and not a sound for twenty minutes.

On VE +1 day, shortage of food compelled us to close, but it was the 'Fellowship' day. We had lunch out, and then took the bus and our tea to Pateley Bridge,[63] and walked five miles in glorious sunshine, and most of the way by the river. We stopped for tea, and afterwards we 'drew near' and with 'Loved with Everlasting Love', 'The King of Love my Shepherd is,' and the 103rd Psalm, and a message—we thanked Him who daily loadeth us with benefits.

The British Flag, July/August 1945

Rebuilding

The end of the war also led SASRA and many individual Christians to consider their future service for God.

As 'V Day' approaches, our members are, one by one, writing to say they believe they are being led of God to Evangelistic and Missionary Service, while some have indicated their desire to become Scripture Readers.

---

60 1 Corinthians 15:57.

61 2 Samuel 23:12.

62 Exodus 15:1.

63 Pateley Bridge is in North Yorkshire on the River Nidd.

As we have said on previous occasions, as soon as peace is proclaimed and demobilisation commences, the Association will need some forty to fifty young men as Readers to take the place of those, both at home and abroad, who will be retiring—some to resume their pastoral duties, having come to the Association for the duration of the War only, and others, whose period of overseas service has long since expired.

As it is realised that the War period has prevented as deep a study of the Scripture on the part of many who otherwise would have delved more deeply therein, it has been made possible for a Bible Correspondence Course, free of charge, to be available to any Ex Service Scripture Readers desiring to avail themselves of it during the first two years of their service as such.

Ready, May/June 1945

The whole nation, from the King down to the labourer, has testified to their thankfulness to God for His overwhelming mercies and deliverances which we, as a people, have deserved so little. May we not in the days to come, forget Him and turn everyone to his own way, pursuing selfish and worldly aims, and thus turn our backs upon God. It is realised by all thoughtful people that the time of peace making and peace keeping will be fraught with great difficulties and many dangers; but let us now consider especially the case as it applies to our Readers.

In war time men, who are faced with the possibility of death or wounds, naturally have their thoughts turned to the world which lies beyond this present one, and to eternal issues. Speaking broadly they are more inclined to give ear to the Readers' message, the message of eternal salvation through faith in the atoning sacrifice of the only Saviour, Jesus Christ.

With the coming of peace, however, the picture is changed. Demobilisation, the return to home and family, and the prospects of permanent civil employment, naturally fill the man's thoughts and tend to crowd out thoughts of the world to come, and to obliterate spiritual impressions which in wartime have made themselves felt upon his mind. In so far as this is the case, the task of the Reader is made more difficult by the prospects of a long and lasting peace, but his duties are as urgent as ever.

There is no release in his warfare against sin and the devil, or in the necessity for him to press eternal issues upon his hearers, however much or however little they may be inclined to respond. For it is appointed unto every man to die and after death the judgment[64] and none can know what a day may bring forth. Let none of us be slack in upholding the Readers both by prayer and by gift. Let none of us think that because the war in the West is over, the work of the Reader, and the necessity for that work has become any the less important. We may be certain that Satan will be active in seeking to snatch away the seeds which have been sown, and that the thorns will spring up more abundantly than ever to choke the growing wheat. It is incumbent upon us to gird up the loins of our mind[65] and to press forward on the straight and narrow way. May the Lord of might and God of Grace strengthen each

---

64 Hebrews 9:28.

65 1 Peter 1:13. 'Gird up the loins' is a picture of being ready for action.

one of us, both Readers and friends, in fulfilling His most holy will.

The British Flag, July/August 1945

Six years ago, when within a quarter of a century Germany had once again plunged the world into war, His Majesty the King called the Nation to prayer. At the close of his message His Majesty said: 'We can only do right as we see right, and reverently commit our cause to God.'

On pondering over these words, and as we look back upon those tragic six years, we can surely see how the Lord did undertake our cause and enabled the Allies to do the right as they saw the right, until Victory was finally accorded and peace throughout the world once more vouchsafed.

Truly, we ought to acclaim with the Psalmist: 'Not unto us, O Lord, not unto us, but unto Thy Name give glory.'[66]

For other victories, too, we would not be unmindful to render Him praise, for many a spiritual battle has been fought and won in the hearts and lives of fellows and girls, as they have faced up to the forces of evil, little of which they realized existed, until they met it for the first time on joining the Services, but with Paul they have been able to say, 'Thanks be to God which giveth us the victory, through our Lord Jesus Christ.'[67]

Many too there are, who, during their Service career, have come to know Jesus as their Saviour and Lord. For such we specially pray, for on their return to civilian life some will, for conscience sake, feel that they cannot go

---

66 Psalm 115:1.

67 1 Corinthians 15:57.

back to their former employment, but as they trust in the Lord and honour Him, they will surely find He will undertake—'Them that honour Me, I will honour'[68] is as valid to-day as ever.

Others, no doubt, having seen the need of Christian witness in other lands in which they have been stationed, may be turning their thoughts in the direction of missionary service, while yet others may be thinking of the need of evangelizing the personnel of the peace-time Army and Air Force. For all such we pray that they may truly understand what the will of the Lord is, and having been shown His will be ready to place themselves unreservedly at their Lord's disposal.

Ready, September/October 1945

A subject which is very much upon our hearts just now is the return to 'Civilian life' of those who have so very much enjoyed and have been helped by the Christian comradeship which a Service career affords, and how best we may be able to help them. Some have already written since they have been demobbed, saying how much they are missing the fellowship and opportunities of service which they have so recently enjoyed. Others have even said that they are finding it harder to live the Christian life as a civilian than when serving in the Forces.

As far as our fellow-members are concerned, we want to be of help. May we suggest, therefore that you never fail to have your 'QT' regularly morning by morning before setting off upon your day's appointment. Many of you will be setting up a home of your own; in doing

---

68 1 Samuel 2:30.

so, may we venture to suggest that family worship should have its regular place, using, it may be the SU portion day by day, maintaining thereby a definite contact with the Association. Many, no doubt, would like to know of any other Members who may be living in or near their home town, with a view to coming together periodically as was usual when serving.

After the last War, 1914-1918, there were many such gatherings known as Old Members' Branches. To form such again, it will be necessary for someone to take the initiative by inviting any others whom they may know of to meet for prayer and talk things over. Headquarters will be pleased to co-operate as much as possible and it is hoped that many will write giving us their home address and signifying that they are desirous of contacting others who may be living in their vicinity.

Another way of making contact is by wearing in one's buttonhole the Association's Badge. This is in the form of a small enamelled shield and may be obtained from Headquarters at a cost of 1/6.

Old Members' Branches should afford splendid opportunities for a continuance of a virile Christian witness in civilian life, which so many of you have engaged in and enjoyed whilst serving. How splendid it would be if every town possessed its own 'Ex-Forces Christian Witness Team!'

Ready, November/December 1945

10. Postscript

A review by SASRA's Chairman of the work of the Association during the War Years

Though it had been evident for some considerable time that Japan was cracking, yet the acceptance of unconditional surrender came with dramatic and unexpected suddenness. Rarely have two such powerful and warlike nations, like Germany and Japan, been reduced to utter defeat and impotence in such a startling manner. Well may our country and Empire humbly acknowledge the mercies of our God, and thank Him that He has not dealt with us after our sins, nor rewarded us according to our iniquities.[69] While we might have feared with justice the afflicting hand of a neglected God, He has dealt with us in loving-kindness, mercy and patience.

May we never forget that the patience and goodness of God is intended to lead man to repentance,[70] and we as a nation have much to repent: worldliness, hardness of heart and contempt of His word and commandments are our prevailing national sins, and it is doubtless due to the earnest and faithful prayers of His servants, that we are enabled this day to praise Him with joyful lips.

Another mercy which we should note is that, although this war has lasted six years, as against four and a quarter years of the last war; although the numbers mobilised are greatly in excess of those serving in 1914-1918, and although the weapons and methods of war have grown

---

69 Psalm 103:10.

70 Romans 2:4.

more powerful, indiscriminating and destructive since 1918, yet our casualties have been scarcely one half of those incurred during the last war. Our grateful hearts should exclaim, 'Bless the Lord, O my soul, and forget not all His benefits.'[71]

Let us now glance in retrospect over the work of our Association during the past six years, and record with thankfulness what we have been enabled to achieve, all too little that it has been.

Before the war, when the so called 'Militia' was called up, and hundreds of thousands of young men became liable for military training, every endeavour was made through the various churches to let these men know of the Association and how it could help them in their new and unaccustomed life. It was not long before war was declared and general conscription enforced: a state of affairs which threw immense responsibilities, accompanied with great opportunities, upon the Association.

The need for many more Readers was instantaneous, and it may be stated here that during the past seven years or so, not a single suitable candidate has been refused, and by efforts of our loyal and devoted supporters every financial need has been met. It soon became obvious that the methods which were so successful in the last war, were not suitable for this one. Then the erection of stationary huts in fixed camps met a great need and was blessed greatly. During this war, owing to the constant changes in the location of the troops, this method had but a limited usefulness, though the huts erected at Blandford,

---

71 Psalm 103:2.

St Athan and Sarafand, served their purpose and were greatly appreciated.

To meet the changed conditions of this war it was decided to open at all suitable centres, Rest Rooms in charge of Readers and their wives or of Lady workers, where the spiritual work of the Association could be carried on. These Rest Rooms were hired premises where (as a rule) light refreshments could be obtained, and which could be given up at short notice, should conditions render it necessary. In all a total of 35 Rest Rooms opened, and the Association was most fortunate in obtaining the voluntary services of Mr Montague Goodman and Mr Robert A Laidlaw to supervise this branch of its work. These gentlemen proceeded to France early in the war, to start Hut and Rest Room work with the British Expeditionary Force.

The disasters in France and the evacuation of the BEF from Dunkirk brought this to a rapid close: but we record with thankfulness that none of our Readers, 12 in number, who were serving with the BEF lost their lives or suffered anything worse than risks and loss of possessions.

Meanwhile the Middle East made great demands for Readers and 12 in all were sent out there under Mr St.Clair, a gentleman who knew Egypt well. That country, the Desert, Palestine and Persia-Iraq, absorbed all the Readers that could be sent. It was at Sarafand in Palestine that the Cluden Hut was erected, by the generosity of Irish friends, and proved most useful.

In due course N Africa, Crete, Tunis and Italy required the services of Readers, and the Reader in Crete went through terrific adventures and came out safely; but we have to record with sorrow that later on this Reader Mr Howe lost his life on his way home when his ship was torpedoed by a German submarine. We remember with gratitude his services in N Africa and Crete, and thank God that he was the only Reader lost through enemy action; the good hand of God in protecting our many Readers is a subject for praise. In other parts of the Empire Readers were serving in India, Ceylon, Singapore, Gibraltar, Malta etc. The maximum number of Readers serving at any one time was 178 men and 20 ladies.

With the conscription of women a new problem arose, for the need, to present the Gospel to the young women of our land, is alas as necessary and urgent as it is to the men. To meet this pressing need Lady Scripture Readers were enrolled, for service among the ATS and WAAF. To open up this new method of work, immense difficulties had to be overcome, and progress was not made in a day; but the system is working now as smoothly and efficiently as the older work.

When the long looked for invasion of France took place, it was not long before a team of 10 Readers was working under our staunch friend and helper, Mr R A Laidlaw, in FM Sir B Montgomery's[72] Army Group, where they did good work. When Mr Laidlaw was compelled to return to New Zealand on urgent business affairs, he was succeeded by Mr Taylor, a tried and most efficient worker.

In India, Major Lee-Spratt has been carrying on our work in that country, Ceylon[73] and Burma, with well-

---

72 Sir Bernard Montgomery (later Viscount Montgomery of Alamein) (1887-1976) commanded the 8th Army in North Africa and Italy 1942-43, was Commander of Ground forces for the invasion of Normandy (1944) and then commanded 21st Army Group in North West Europe 1944-45.

73 Ceylon is now Sri Lanka.

known energy and zeal, in the face of his great difficulties. Efforts to get Readers into Burma for work among our troops there, were hindered greatly, but a Reader got into Rangoon at last, and is working there most happily.

In reviewing the work of the Readers in this brief manner, we must not overlook the work done by the administrative staff both at Home and Abroad. Apart from the increase of work caused by the largely increased staff of Readers, all sorts of difficulties had to be faced and overcome, such as the arrangement with the War Office for passages and the many questions which arose due to the employment of so many Readers with the armies in the Field.

Reliefs and replacements caused much work and anxiety, while as the war progressed and the food conditions at home got progressively more difficult, the problems of our Rest Rooms too often became almost insoluble. It has to be remembered that all this administrative work had to be carried out with shortage of staff, which at times became acute, owing to the impossibility of obtaining replacements. To Colonel Macaulay and his staff in London a large debt of gratitude is due, for without efficient administration at the Bases, the work of the Readers would have been frustrated in large measure.

Senior officers have been almost universally sympathetic and helpful and we would acknowledge especially the assistance given by FM Sir Harold Alexander,[74] FM Sir Bernard Montgomery, Lieut.-General Sir William

---

74 Sir Harold Alexander (later Earl Alexander of Tunis) (1891-1969) was Commander in Chief of Middle East 1942-43, then commanded 18th Army Group in Tunisia and 15th Army Group for the invasion of Italy. He was Commander in Chief of all Allied forces in Italy 1944-45.

Dobbie,[75] Lieut.-General Sir Arthur Smith,[76] among a multitude of good friends. Special thanks are due also to the Chaplain-Generals, Chaplains-in-Chief and their respective staffs. Without their cordial help it would not have been possible to carry on, and we are glad to record the special debt of gratitude, which we owe to them.

With the end of the war it must not be thought that the work of the Association becomes less important or less pressing. For a very long time to come large forces will be maintained on the Continent and abroad, and the temptations to which the soldier is exposed are greater in peace time than in war. How we can meet our obligations best is a matter calling for prayer, thought and wise planning.

One of our most urgent needs is that for young Readers. During the war the provision of Readers for service in the field or in the tropics has been a constant difficulty, owing to nearly every young man being called up for Government service. All honour is due to those middle-aged Readers who have carried on under such trying conditions. We would desire our friends to pray that with demobilisation younger men may come forward called to this work and with a heartfelt desire to minister in spiritual things to their comrades who are still serving, and we would remind our friends of the urgency and importance of the great work which lies ahead.

---

75 Sir William Dobbie (1879-1964) was Governor and Commander in Chief of Malta 1940-42 and then President of SASRA 1947-67.

76 Sir Arthur Smith (1890-1977) was General Officer commanding London district (1942-44) and then Commander in Chief of Persia and Iraq (1944-45). He was Chairman of SASRA 1948-67 and then President 1967-77.

Truly the labourers are all too few, but we humbly thank God for what He has enabled the Association to do for His honour and glory and for the salvation of souls during the past 107 years, and not least of all during the past six years. He is the same and changes not, and is ever our Refuge and Strength.

The British Flag, November/December 1945

11. Acronyms

21 AG	21st Army Group. Operated in North West Europe between June 1944 and August 1945. It consisted primarily of the First Canadian Army and the British Second Army, but at various times also included additional American, British, Canadian and Polish forces.
AA	Anti-Aircraft.
ACG	Assistant Chaplain-General.
ASR	Army Scripture Reader.
ASR&SACA	Army Scripture Readers and Soldiers' and Airmen's Christian Association.
ASR&SFS	Army Scripture Readers and Soldiers' Friend Society.
ATS	Auxiliary Territorial Service of the Army (Women's service). Formed in 1938 and merged into the Women's Royal Army Corps in 1949.
BB	Black Board meeting. Meetings where members shared Bible texts.
BBC	British Broadcasting Corporation.
BEF	British Expeditionary Force.
BLA	British Liberation Army. British forces which fought on the Western Front between the invasion of Normandy and the end of the war. In August 1945, it became the British Army of the Rhine (BAOR).
CO	Commanding Officer.
C.of.E	Church of England.
CVWW	Council of Voluntary War Workers
FM	Field Marshal, the highest rank in the British Army (5 star General).
GHQ	General Headquarters.
Gnr	Gunner, Royal Artillery equivalent of a Private.

HGS	Honorary General Secretary.
HMS	His Majesty's Ship.
LAC	Leading Aircraftman.
LCM	London City Mission, founded in 1835.
MO	Medical Officer.
NCO	Non-Commissioned Officer.
NYLC	National Young Life Campaign, founded in 1911.
OC	Officer Commanding or Officer in Command.
PoW	Prisoner of War.
Pte	Private.
QT	Quiet Time. Spending time in prayer and Bible reading.
RA	Royal Artillery.
RAF	Royal Air Force.
RASC	Royal Army Service Corps.
REME	Royal Electrical and Mechanical Engineers.
RHQ	Regimental Headquarters.
RSM	Regimental Sergeant Major
SACA	Soldiers' and Airmen's Christian Association.
SASRA	Soldiers' and Airmen's Scripture Readers Association.
SCA	Soldiers' Christian Association.
SCF	Senior Chaplain to the Forces.
SCM	Student Christian Movement, founded in 1889.
SGM	Scripture Gift Mission, founded in 1888, now known as Lifewords.
SP	Service Police.
SR	Scripture Reader.
SU	Scripture Union. Formed in 1867 as the Children's Special Service Mission (CSSM). In 1879, it formed the Children's Scripture Union which began issuing Daily Notes in 1923.
Tpr	Trooper, cavalry regiment equivalent of a Private.

USA   United States of America.

USS   United States Ship.

USSR   Union of Soviet Socialist Republics. State which existed between 1922 and 1991 when it divided into a number of republics, the largest being Russia.

V1   German flying bomb also known as 'doodlebugs' or 'buzz bombs.'

V2   German ballistic missile.

VE   Victory Europe.

VJ   Victory Japan.

WAAF   Woman's Auxiliary Air Force. Created in June 1939, became the Women's Royal Air Force in February 1949.

WRNS   Women's Royal Naval Service. First formed in 1917 but disbanded in 1919. Revived in 1939 and integrated into the Royal Navy in 1993.

YLC   See NYLC.

YMCA   Young Men's Christian Association, founded in 1844.

That was SASRA Then … Now …

Our Scripture Readers are still all ex-Service men or women, many having themselves become Christians while serving. They therefore know from first-hand experience the environment in which they work and can relate to and understand those currently serving.

Their warm friendly approach, makes vital use of informal contacts with servicemen and women to build friendships in order to introduce them to the Lord Jesus Christ. Although civilians, they are required to wear uniform for ease of recognition, but carry no rank or privileges.

Working in barrack rooms, detention centres, medical facilities and training units, often in Chaplains Hours, there is ample scope for a ministry that under God's guidance carries the privilege of both sowing and reaping.

Co-operation with Chaplains is seen in various ways. Both in informal and more formal settings it is good to reinforce the common message. Most Scripture Readers and their wives are also able to work among the families and their children and have been greatly used in this sphere.

The unique nature of the Association's ministry has always required close links with Commanding Officers and Chaplains who, under the terms of the Charters, are able to authorise Scripture Readers to visit men and women of the Units. This privilege and responsibility is not afforded to any other Christian organisation or local civilian Church.

Soldiers do not change, neither therefore has the vital work of SASRA changed.

'What has been is what will be, and what has been done is what will be done, and there is nothing new under the sun' (Ecclesiastes 1:9).

Yes I want to **HELP PARTNER** with SASRA's ministry.

☐ **A ONE-OFF GIFT**

☐ **£10 can buy a hard-wearing Bible for a soldier or airman.**

☐ **£50 can fund a Scripture Reader taking the gospel to soldiers/airmen on exercise.**

☐ **£100 can pay for a whole Bible study course.**

☐ **£_____ (please fill in the amount of your choice)**
I enclose my (cash/cheque) donation to sponsor SASRA's work.

☐ **I do not wish to receive an acknowledgement.**

Or if you wish to donate using your credit/debit card please either visit the donate page on the SASRA website **www.sasra.org.uk** or alternatively telephone SASRA HQ on **03000 301302**

☐ **REGULAR GIFT to support the work of SASRA**

☐ **I might be able to invest TIME in my local community to help SASRA's mission, and would like to discuss that with someone**

STANDING ORDER

To _____ Bank PLC _____ Branch _____ Sort Code

Please pay to the account of SASRA, sort code 161926, account number 10139767 the sum of

£ _____ ☐ each month ☐ quarter ☐ half year ☐ annually from my

account number ☐☐☐☐☐☐☐☐

Starting on ☐☐/☐☐ until further notice.

Signature: _____ Date: _____

Boost your donation by 25p of Gift Aid for every £1 you donate

Gift Aid is claimed by the charity from the tax you pay for the current tax year. Your address is needed to identify you as a current UK taxpayer. In order to Gift Aid your donation you must tick the box below.

☐ I want to Gift Aid my donation of £_____ and any donation I make in the future or have made in the past 4 years to the Soldiers' and Airmen's Scripture Readers Association.

I am a UK taxpayer and understand that if I pay less Income Tax and/or Capital Gains Tax than the amount of Gift Aid claimed on all my donations in that tax year it is my responsibility to pay any difference. I will notify SASRA if I wish to cancel this declaration, change my name or address or no longer pay sufficient tax on my income or capital gains.

Signature: _____ Date: _____

(PLEASE RETURN TO SASRA HQ)

Name (Mr/Mrs/Ms/Other): _____

Address: _____

_____ Postcode: _____

Email: _____

GDPR 2018 – SASRA will hold the information you give us for administrative purposes. We will only pass on your contact details to third parties if it is required by law, or in order to provide you with services you have requested.

SASRA Havelock House, Barrack Road, Aldershot, Hampshire GU11 3NP
Telephone: **03000 301302** email: **admin@sasra.org.uk**

www.sasra.org.uk

Registered Charity No 235708 In Scotland SCO 39130
A Company limited by guarantee; registered in England No. 329268

Rough Journal

H. WISBEY / SASRA HQ

The inspirational story of Army Scripture Reader Harry Wisbey with the Suffolk Regiment, Expeditionary Force August–September 1914

Paperback

Publisher: 10 Publishing; 1st Edition 2014

ISBN 978-1-90961-189-4

£4.00

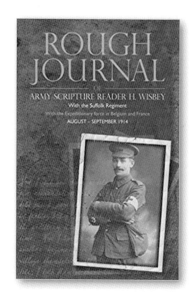

SASRA at the Somme

W. G. RANSLEY

**The War Diaries of
ASR 'Old Bill' Ransley**

ED. SHONA WILKIE

72pp
ISBN 978-1-84625-542-7
Day One Ref SASRAS5427
£6.00

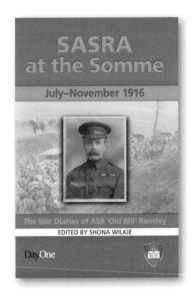

SASRA (The Soldiers' and Airmen's Scripture Readers Association) brings you Old Bill's writings during the Battle of the Somme, from July to November 1916! Old Bill (William Ransley) became an Army Scripture Reader shortly after leaving the army in 1889. Having worked for God in his last six years serving in the army, he decided to dedicate his time and energy to sharing the gospel full time with the men and women of the military. His work saw him sailing off to the hospitals in northern France, where he experienced the bloodbath of the Battle of the Somme through his encounters with injured soldiers from both sides. His journal gives a glimpse of the role of Scripture Readers and sheds light on the message of hope SASRA readers took, and still take, to the men and women of the Armed Forces.

Scripture Reading to the End

ASR William G Ransley and his Gospel witness, France, 1918

ED. BILL NEWTON

100pp
ISBN 978-1-84625-603-5
Day One Ref SCE6035
£6.00

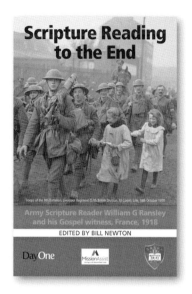

With a deep reliance on and faith in the Lord Jesus Christ, Army Scripture Reader William Ransley takes us into the agony of the Great War and shows us men facing their mortality both with and without Christ. Posted to Boulogne in 1914 and later to the hospitals of Wimereux in Northern France, Ransley faithfully witnessed to those profoundly affected by the war. His honest, gracious testimony and compassion are a challenge to us all. This book takes Ransley's diary and focuses attention on the period when World War One staggered to its brutal and horrifying conclusion in 1918. The need was great: so many souls on both sides, facing a violent entrance into eternity. Yet through it all, Ransley's faith in Christ and unswerving loyalty to speak the truth is the light that shines in encircling darkness.

The Fight of Faith

Lives and testimonies from the battlefield

Compiled and edited by
Colonel P Bray and
Major M Claydon,
SASRA Council.

201pp (Hardback)
ISBN 978-1-95760-890-0
Published by Panoplia
£7.00

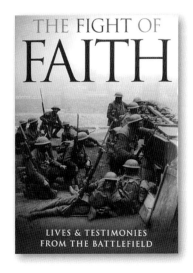

Many an Officer and Serviceman who were committed Christians have testified that they have proved the power of God to keep and help them in their military duty on operations. The Fight of Faith brings together for the first time fifteen such testimonies; from Guardsman to Generals, serving from Malta to Mogadishu in civil and world war. They all found the promises given in The Bible to be true and answers to prayer to be real even in these testing circumstances.

SASRA—
The Lord's Prayer—
Equipping Disciples to Serve

Learning from Jesus how to talk to His Father

PAUL BLACKHAM

With illustrative stories from SASRA Scripture Readers and Area Representatives

ED. SHONA WILKIE

128pp
ISBN 978-1-84625-559-5
Day One Ref SASRALP5595
£6.00

Rev. Blackham and SASRA bring you a study of the basic pattern of the Lord's Prayer, helping you to learn from Jesus, the Eternal Son, how to speak to His Father, who is enthroned in the highest heaven. For messed-up people like us to speak to the most holy Father in the highest level of reality is utterly impossible—but because of Jesus, it is possible. And knowing how to talk to our heavenly Father as Jesus did is the key to knowing life and peace, even in the most terrible circumstances. Each line of the prayer is illustrated through stories told by current Scripture Readers and Area Representatives of encounters with men and women of the Armed Forces as they have seen the outworking of this prayer in SASRA's ministry. May this book encourage you to speak to the Father of our Lord Jesus, and to remember our soldiers, airmen and airwomen in prayer.

Other SASRA books

Operation Salvation

DAVID MURRAY

96pp
ISBN 978-1-84625-629-5
Day One Ref SASRAOS6295
£6.00

This is a gripping tale of bravado, booze, battles and at times bitter failures. In an action-packed life David Murray escaped dead-end jobs, Glasgow knife-gangs and bullets in Northern Ireland.

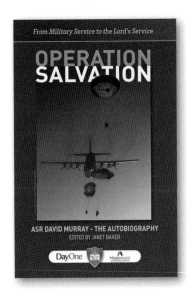

His autobiography is a well-paced and plain-speaking account of a man constantly on the move—until the day God Himself finally caught up with him. This is a great book of memories charting Glasgow and Army life in the 60s and 70s. But it's much more than social history.

"It's a wonderful testimony to God's surprising mercy and power in unlikely places and people. A book to read and to give away."
ANDY HUNTER, FIEC Scotland & North of England Director

The Guardsman

By Guardsman George Venables
Signaller in the 3rd Battalion
Coldstream Guards
May 1915 – January 1919

ED. JAMIE CAMPBELL

136pp
ISBN 978-1-84625-650-9
Day One Ref SASRATG6509
£6.00

If you are familiar with SASRA's
World War One 'Trilogy' you will
be conversant with a Scripture Reader's battlefield. Changing-up,
SASRA has now overseen the publication of a book that details
war through the eyes of a practising Christian who signed-up
ahead of time, did his duty—and survived. With modest tones
and dry humour, *The Guardsman* gets you right up to the coal
face of global conflict, spiritual tension and personal loss. Above
all, *The Guardsman* demonstrates in the furnace that faith in God
is possible and, frankly, essential.